MW01628666

1973

WHAT A YEAR IT WAS!

A walk back in time...

To

From

FLICKBACK

Dedicated to
the Intrepid Investigative Reporters

Managing Editor/Publisher • Art Worthington
Design, Writing & Research • Peter Hess

www.FLICKBACK.com
(800) 541-3533

Contents

Arts & Entertainment

Inspired by his '60s acting work in several influential Spaghetti Westerns, **Clint Eastwood** directs his second feature, *High Plains Drifter*, casting himself as a nameless stranger who drifts into an isolated mining town where he metes out violent justice to miscreants. Before his departure, he demands that the town be painted blood-red and branded 'Hell.'

An even more offbeat Western, *Westworld* features **Yul Brynner** in a sci-fi tale of androids run amok in a futuristic Western-themed amusement park. Decades later, it will spawn the popular HBO *Westworld* TV series.

Sam Peckinpah, known for the explicit violence in his films, directs *Pat Garrett and Billy the Kid*. **James Coburn** and **Kris Kristofferson** star in the revisionist Western, memorable for **Bob Dylan's** music, especially the song "Knockin' on Heaven's Door."

Movies

Films That Make a Mark

A number of 1973 movies pack a punch that reverberates into the present day. Near the top of the heap is director **George Roy Hill's** con artist caper, *The Sting*. **Paul Newman** and **Robert Redford** display a bantering chemistry as a pair of depression-era grifters setting their sights on a Chicago mob boss (**Robert Shaw**), with briskly entertaining results. *The Sting* is a critical and commercial bonanza, nabbing the Best Picture Oscar and six others.

Redford delivers again in another award-winner, the romantic drama *The Way We Were*. In his college days, his character is smitten with a political activist, portrayed by **Barbra Streisand**. Years later, they begin a torrid affair against a taut political backdrop. The soundtrack album featuring Streisand's performance of the title track is a smash hit, just like the movie.

Crime dramas captivate, including director **Martin Scorsese's** tale of small-time mob hustlers in New York's Little Italy, *Mean Streets*. **Robert DeNiro** and **Harvey Keitel** sizzle in an influential film that marks the arrival of Scorsese as one of the modern-era crime genre's founding originals.

Al Pacino battles crooks and corruption in *Serpico*, an account of real-life NYPD cop Frank Serpico's career. When his colleagues fail to convince him to take payoffs, they set him up to receive a gunshot wound during a drug bust.

A pair of Navy shore patrolmen are ordered to escort a court-martialed fellow sailor to prison in **Hal Ashby's** film, *The Last Detail*, with hilarious results. **Jack Nicholson** and **Randy Quaid** star. And a big cast of up-and-coming actors, including **Richard Dreyfuss** and **Ron Howard**, **Harrison Ford** and **Candy Clark**, feature in the **George Lucas** coming-of-age comedy/drama, *American Graffiti*, nostalgically set in 1962.

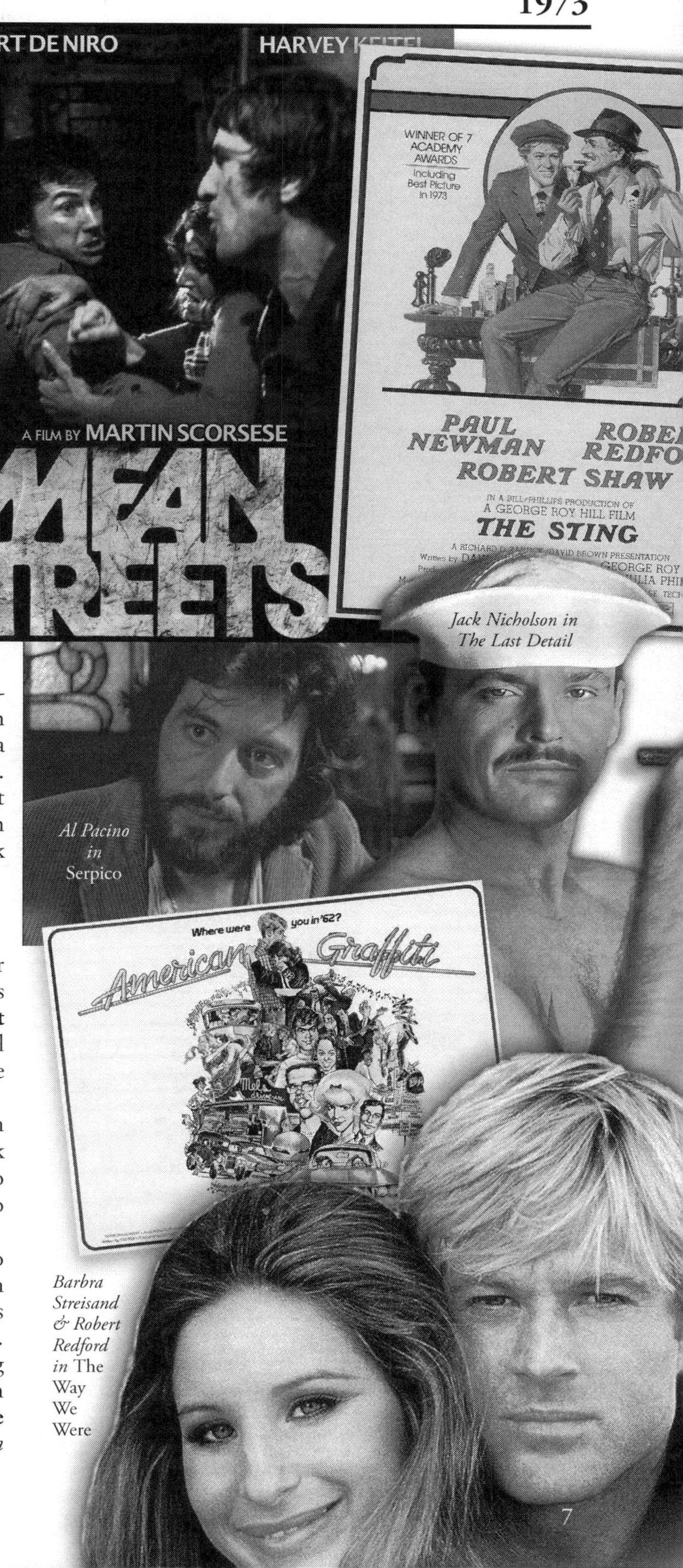

Jack Nicholson in The Last Detail

Al Pacino in Serpico

Barbra Streisand & Robert Redford in The Way We Were

WHAT'S PLAYING AT THE MOVIES

Charley Varrick
Charlotte's Web
Cinderella Liberty
The Day of the Dolphin
THE DAY OF THE JACKAL
THE DON IS DEAD
Don't Look Now
ELECTRA GLIDE IN BLUE
Emperor of the North Pole
ENTER the DRAGON
The Friends of Eddie Coyle
GODSPELL
Heavy Traffic
The Hireling
THE HOMECOMING
The ICEMAN COMETH
Jesus Christ Superstar
Jonathan Livingston Seagull
Kid Blue
THE LAST AMERICAN HERO
THE LAUGHING POLICEMAN

BADLANDS
BANG THE DRUM SLOWLY
BLOOD of the DRAGON
Blue Blood
BLUME IN LOVE
Breezy
CAHILL U.S. MARSHALL

The LAST of SHEILA
LIVE and LET DIE
The Long Goodbye
LOST HORIZON
The MACKINTOSH MAN
MAGNUM FORCE
The NEPTUNE FACTOR
Night Flight from Moscow
NIGHT WATCH
Oklahoma Crude
O LUCKY MAN!
The PAPER CHASE
PAPER MOON
PAPILLON
SAVE the TIGER
SCARECROW
SCORPIO
THE SEVEN-UPS
SISTERS
SLEEPER
Steelyard Blues
The Thief Who Came to Dinner
The Three Musketeers
A Touch of Class
The Train Robbers
WALKING TALL

The Academy Awards

"And The Winner Is..."

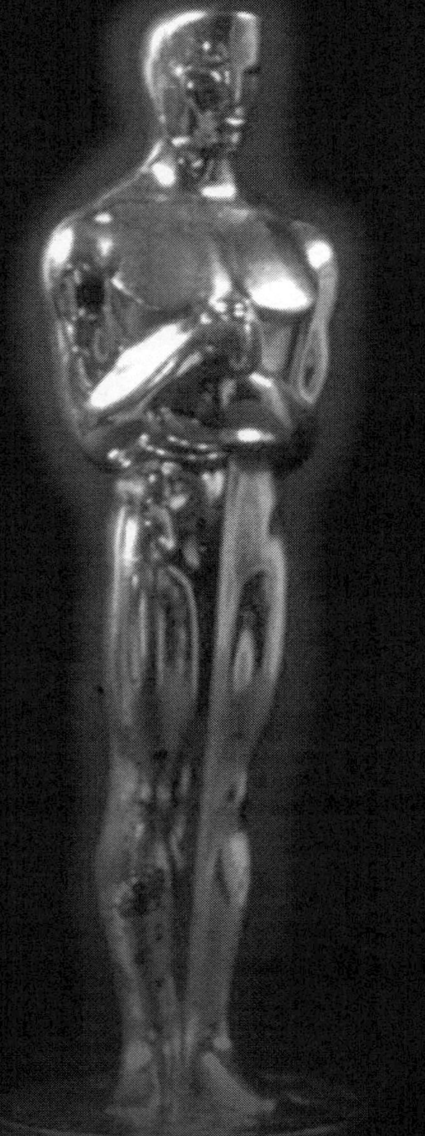

Oscars® Presented in 1973 *(for 1972 Films)*

Joel Grey

BEST PICTURE
THE GODFATHER

BEST ACTOR
MARLON BRANDO,
The Godfather

BEST ACTRESS
LIZA MINELLI,
Cabaret

BEST DIRECTOR
BOB FOSSE,
Cabaret

BEST SUPPORTING ACTOR
JOEL GREY, *Cabaret*

BEST SUPPORTING ACTRESS
EILEEN HECKART, *Butterflies Are Free*

BEST SONG
"THE MORNING AFTER," *The Poseidon Adventure*

1973 Favorites *(Oscars® Presented in 1974)*

Glenda Jackson

BEST PICTURE
THE STING

BEST ACTOR
JACK LEMMON,
Save the Tiger

BEST ACTRESS
GLENDA JACKSON,
A Touch of Class

BEST DIRECTOR
GEORGE ROY HILL,
The Sting

BEST SUPPORTING ACTOR
JOHN HOUSEMAN, *The Paper Chase*

BEST SUPPORTING ACTRESS
TATUM O'NEAL, *Paper Moon*

BEST SONG
"THE WAY WE WERE," *The Way We Were*

45th Annual Academy Awards Ceremony

• March 27, 1973 •
Dorothy Chandler Pavilion

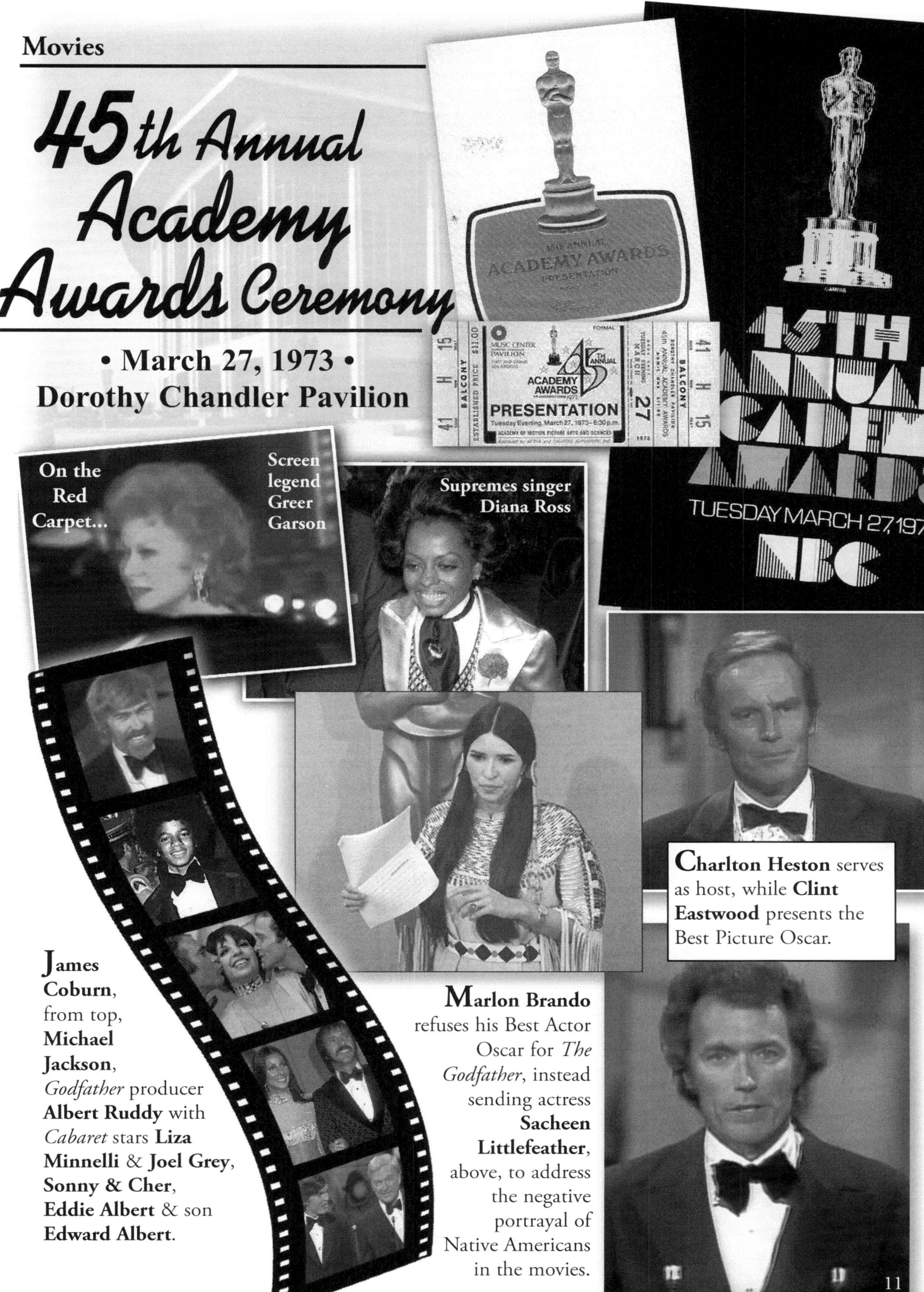

On the Red Carpet...

Screen legend Greer Garson

Supremes singer Diana Ross

Charlton **Heston** serves as host, while **Clint Eastwood** presents the Best Picture Oscar.

James **Coburn**, from top, **Michael Jackson**, *Godfather* producer **Albert Ruddy** with *Cabaret* stars **Liza Minnelli** & **Joel Grey**, **Sonny & Cher**, **Eddie Albert** & son **Edward Albert**.

Marlon **Brando** refuses his Best Actor Oscar for *The Godfather*, instead sending actress **Sacheen Littlefeather**, above, to address the negative portrayal of Native Americans in the movies.

The 31st GOLDEN GLOBE AWARDS

Honoring the best in film and television for 1973 and bestowed on January 26, 1974 by members of the Hollywood Foreign Press Association

BEST MOTION PICTURE - Drama
The Exorcist

Comedy or Musical
American Graffiti

BEST ACTOR - Drama
Al Pacino
Serpico

BEST ACTRESS - Drama
Marsha Mason
Cinderella Liberty

BEST ACTOR - Comedy/Musical
George Segal
A Touch of Class

BEST ACTRESS - Comedy/Musical
Glenda Jackson
A Touch of Class

BEST SUPPORTING ACTOR
John Houseman
Thr Paper Chase

BEST SUPPORTING ACTRESS
Linda Blair
The Exorcist

BEST DIRECTOR
William Friedkin
The Exorcist

SOME LIKE IT HOT!

An 'X' rating is designed to serve as a caution to audiences that a film may contain prurient material. But for some, these examples of "porno chic" are an enticing lure.

Geogina Spelvin and **Harry Reems** star in *The Devil in Miss Jones*, an adult film which has gained a reputation as a classic of the "Golden Age of Porn." Filmed in a fruit-packing plant, it vividly depicts wild sex in the afterlife. Reems makes another appearance as a deranged Vietnam vet in the disturbing horror/porn *Forced Entry*, reviled for its scenes of sexual violence.

Porn entrepreneurs the **Mitchell Brothers** follow up their 1972 movie, *Behind the Green Door*, with *Resurrection of Eve*. Both films feature adult film super-star **Marilyn Chambers**. Another 1973 adult film, *The New Comers*, is deemed obscene by the courts and banned from mainstream theatrical release in New York, California, Colorado and Georgia—a fate shared by *Behind the Green Door*.

Truffaut and Bisset in Day for Night.

1973 is a bountiful year for international cinema, with a number of extraordinarily influential foreign films leaving enduring legacies.

From French director/writer/producer **Francois Truffaut** comes *Day for Night*. **Jacqueline Bisset**, **Jean-Pierre Léaud** and Truffaut himself star in a chronicling of life on and off a film set. The movie's title refers to a camera filter trick to make daytime shots appear as if they had been filmed at night.

Highly regarded Swedish auteur **Ingmar Bergman** creates *Scenes from a Marriage*, a distinctly personal telling of the disintegration of his own marriage, spread over 6 hour-long episodes. **Liv Ullmann** and **Erland Josephson** play the stressed couple.

Rutger Hauer has his debut in *Turkish Delight*, directed by **Paul Verhoeven**. One of the most successful films in the history of Dutch cinema, **Monique van de Ven** also features in the erotic drama.

Rutger Hauer

du 10 au 25 MAI

The 26th Annual Cannes Film Festival takes place in May, 1973. ***Godspell*** *by director* **David Greene** *opens the festival, while* **Sidney Furie's** ***Lady Sings the Blues*** *is the closer. Renowned actress* **Ingrid Bergman** *heads the jury.*

Joanne Woodward *and* ***Paul Newman*** *at Cannes.*

GRAND PRIX DU FESTIVAL INTERNATIONAL DU FILM

The Hireling by Alan Bridges

Scarecrow by Jerry Schatzberg

GRAND PRIX SPÉCIAL DU JURY

The Mother and the Whore
by Jean Eustache

BEST ACTRESS

Joanne Woodward
The Effect of Gamma Rays on Man-in-the-Moon Marigolds

BEST ACTOR

Giancarlo Giannini
Love & Anarchy

BRUCE LEE may be the most influential martial artist of all time. His Hong Kong and Hollywood-produced films elevate the traditional fight film to new heights of popularity and ignite a surge of interest in the martial arts. His blockbuster early '70s films include ***The Big Boss***, ***Fist of Fury***, ***Way of the Dragon*** (directed and written by Lee) and ***Enter the Dragon***.

Tragically, Lee dies in 1973, at the age of 32 from diagnosed cerebral edema. ***Game of Death*** remains an unfinished film project, later released in a couple of different "mashup" versions.

Horror & SCI-FI

And Now the Screaming Starts!
Battle for the Planet of the Apes
The Crazies
The Creeping Flesh
Dark Place
The Exorcist
Fantastic Planet
The House in Nightmare Park
The Legend of Hell House
Soylent Green
Theatre of Blood
The Vault of Horror
The Wicker Man

Memorable Lines

SAVE THE TIGER

Myra: *Are you OK? Do you want something?*
Harry Stoner: *Yes. I want that girl in a Cole Porter song. I wanna see Lena Horne at the Cotton Club - hear Billie Holiday sing "Fine and Mellow" - walk in that kind of rain that never washes perfume away. I wanna be in love with something. Anything. Just the idea. A dog, a cat. Anything. Just something.*

The LAST DETAIL

Mulhall: *We'd better catch that train.*
Buddusky: *We still got time for a beer.*
Mulhall: *Now wait a minute, man...*
Meadows: *I ain't old enough.*
Buddusky: *Ain't old enough for what?*
Meadows: *For a beer.*
Buddusky: *Everybody's old enough for a beer. Ain't that right, Mule?*
Mulhall: *Yeah.*

THE PAPER CHASE

Charles Kingsfield: *Mr. Hart, here is a dime. Take it, call your mother, and tell her there is serious doubt about you ever becoming a lawyer.*
James T. Hart: *You... are a son of a bitch, Kingsfield!*
Charles Kingsfield: *Mr. Hart! That is the most intelligent thing you've said today. You may take your seat.*

The STING

Henry Gondorff: *You not gonna stick around for your share?*
Johnny Hooker: *Nah. I'd only blow it.*

Johnny Hooker: *He's not as tough as he thinks.*
Henry Gondorff: *Neither are we.*

Henry Gondorff: *Tough luck, Lonnehan. But that's what you get for playing with your head up your ass!*

Louise Coleman: *If I didn't know you better, I'd swear you had some class!*

The Top-Grossing 1973 Movies

1. *The Exorcist*
2. *The Sting*
3. *American Graffiti*
4. *Papillon*
5. *The Way We Were*
6. *Magnum Force*
7. *Last Tango in Paris*
8. *Paper Moon*
9. *Live and Let Die*
10. *The Devil in Miss Jones*

Ryan O'Neal, Tatum O'Neal in Paper Moon

Progress, Exploitation or Both?

An explosion of so-called "**BLAXPLOITATION**" movies proves a popular draw for '70s audiences, but they create a cause for concern among some. On the upside, they provide opportunities for featuring African Americans in leading film roles. At the same time, they raise questions about the continuing negative depiction of stereotyped Black characters in popular culture.

BLAXPLOITATION 1973

- Black Caesar
- Blackenstein
- Cleopatra Jones
- Coffy
- Five on the Black Hand Side
- Hell Up in Harlem
- Scream Blacula Scream
- Slaughter's Big Rip-Off
- Super Fly T.N.T.

PASSINGS

LEX BARKER, 54 ACTOR ★ JOE E. BROWN, 80 ACTOR ★ LON CHANEY, JR, 67 ACTOR ★ NOEL COWARD, 73 PLAYWRIGHT, ACTOR ★ JOHN FORD, 79 DIRECTOR ★ LAURENCE HARVEY, 45 ACTOR ★ ANNA MAGNANI, 65 ACTRESS ★ ARTHUR FREED, 78 PRODUCER ★ BETTY GRABLE, 56 ACTRESS ★ WILLIAM INGE, 60 WRITER ★ VERONICA LAKE, 50 ACTRESS ★ EDWARD G. ROBINSON, 79 ACTOR ★ ROBERT RYAN, 63 ACTOR

Edward G. Robinson

BORN IN 1973 ★

Adrien Brody

KATE BECKINSDALE ★ ADRIEN BRODY ★ NEVE CAMPBELL ★ DAVE CHAPELLE ★ NEIL PATRICK HARRIS ★ JULIETTE LEWIS ★ SETH MACFARLANE ★ ROSE McGOWAN ★ JIM PARSONS ★ PAUL WALKER ★ KRISTEN WIIG

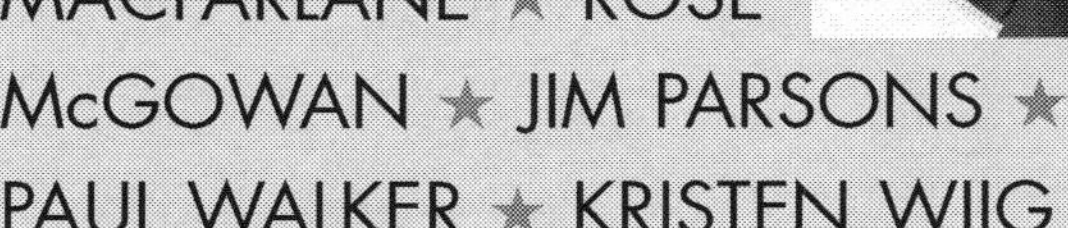

THE TOP BOX OFFICE STARS

Steve McQueen

Clint Eastwood
Ryan O'Neal
Steve McQueen
Burt Reynolds
Robert Redford
Barbra Streisand
Charles Bronson
John Wayne
Marlon Brando
Gene Hackman
Liza Minelli
Roger Moore

Gene Hackman

MOVIE DEBUTS

Danny Aiello
Colleen Camp
John Candy
Joanna Cassidy
Laura Dern
Anthony Edwards
Emilio Estevez
Rutger Hauer
Bernadette Peters
Kathleen Quinlan
Stellan Skarsgard
Carl Weathers

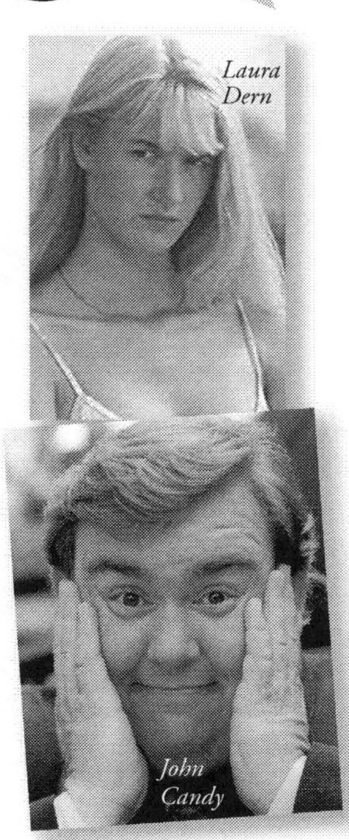

Laura Dern

John Candy

1973 ADVERTISEMENT

Television

The King Live, Worldwide

Elvis Presley takes the world by storm when his January 14th Honolulu concert is broadcast live via satellite and by delay to countries across the globe. ***Aloha from Hawaii*** draws an audience of over a billion, making it the most watched broadcast by an entertainer in TV history. Gyrating in his white rhinestone jumpsuit, Elvis sails through a 22-song set, ranging from the vintage gems "Blue Suede Shoes" and "Hound Dog" to more recent favorites like "My Way" and "Can't Help Falling in Love." He concludes by taking a knee while being draped in a cape.

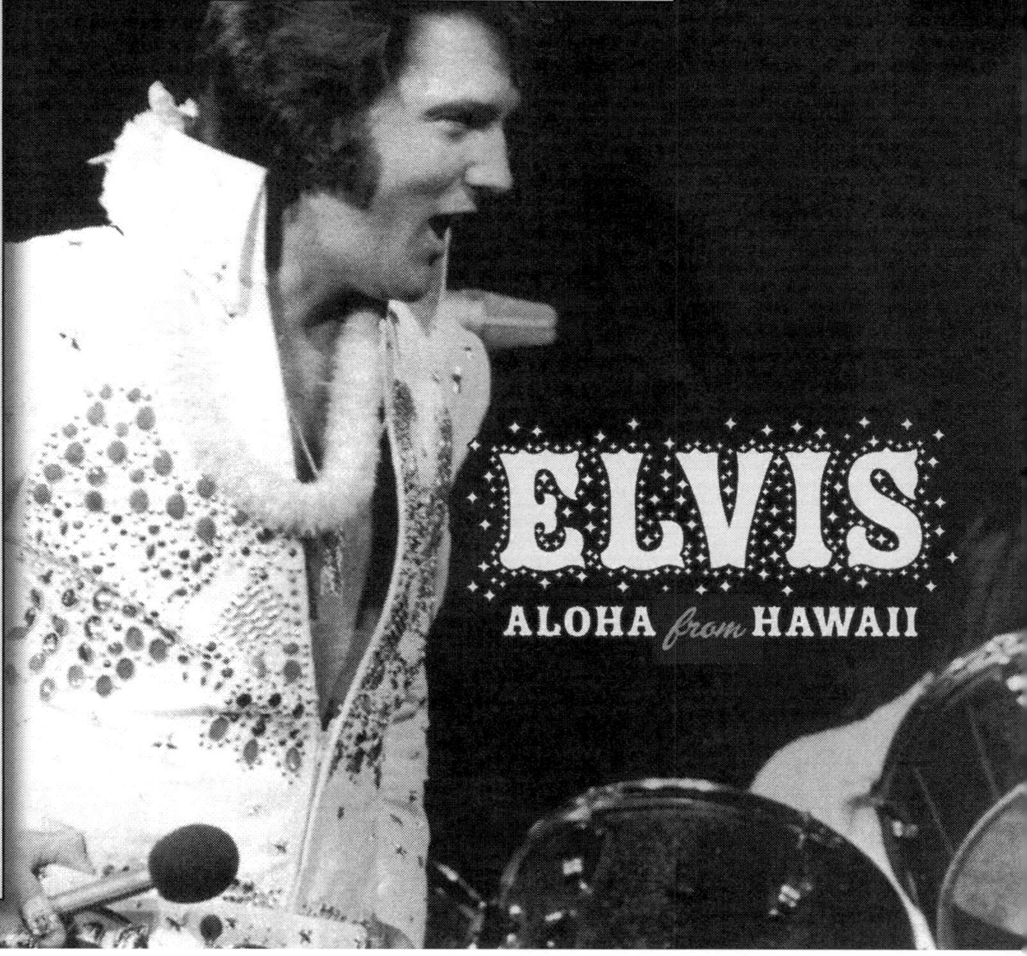

ELVIS
ALOHA *from* HAWAII

— ALL GOOD THINGS MUST END —

First broadcast in 1959, NBC's ***BONANZA*** ends it's 14-season run, making it the 2nd-longest running western series in TV history. **Michael Landon**, **Dan Blocker**, **Lorne Greene** & **Pernell Roberts** *(l-r)* portray the wealthy Cartwright ranch family.

CONCENTRATION, the longest-running daytme game show on NBC, airs it's 3,796th and final episode on March 23rd. First airing in 1958, the show featured various hosts, including **Hugh Downs**, shown below.

NEW SHOWS ON THE TV BLOCK

Barnaby Jones

Police Story

Lotsa Luck

The Young and the Restless

Kojak

The Tomorrow Show with Tom Snyder

Vic Morrow, Chuck Connors and Ed Asner (l-r) in an episode of Police Story

Telly Savalas of Kojak

The U.S. Senate **WATERGATE HEARINGS** dominate daytime television, alternating between CBS, NBC and ABC from May 17th to August 7th.

— SHOWS LEAVING THE AIR —

- ***The Doris Day Show*** **(1968-1973)**
- ***Mission: Impossible*** **(1966-1973)**
- ***The Mod Squad*** **(1968-1973)**
- ***Rowan & Martin's Laugh-In*** **(1968-1973)**

Julie Andrews

The variety special ***Julie on Sesame Street*** airs on ABC in November. **Julie Andrews** is joined by Sesame Street Muppets from the PBS children's series.

1973 PRIMETIME LINEUP

Day	Network	7:00	7:30	8:00	8:30	9:00	9:30	10:00	10:30
SATURDAY	ABC	Local		The Partridge Family	The ABC Suspense Movie			Griff	
	CBS	Local		All in the Family	M*A*S*H	Mary Tyler Moore Show	The Bob Newhart Show	The Carol Burnett Show	
	NBC	Local		Emergency!		NBC Saturday Night at the Movies			
SUNDAY	ABC	Local		The F.B.I.		The ABC Sunday Night Movie			
	CBS	Local	The New Perry Mason		Mannix		60 Minutes		Local
	NBC	Wild Kingdom	The Wonderful World of Disney		The NBC Sunday Mystery Movie (Columbo/McCloud/McMillan & Wife/Hec Ramsey				Local
MONDAY	ABC	Local		The Rookies		Monday Night Football			
	CBS	Local		Gunsmoke		Here's Lucy	New Dick Van Dyke Show	Medical Center	
	NBC	Local		The Magician		NBC Monday Night at the Movies			
TUESDAY	ABC	Local		Happy Days	ABC Tuesday Movie of the Week			Marcus Welby, MD	
	CBS	Local		Maude	Hawaii Five-O		The New CBS Tuesday Night Movies		
	NBC	Local		Adam-12	The NBC Tuesday Mystery Movie (Banacek/Tenafly/Snoop Sisters)			Police Story	
WEDNESDAY	ABC	Local		The Cowboys	ABC Wednesday Movie of the Week			Owen Marshall, Counselor at Law	
	CBS	Local		The Sonny & Cher Comedy Hour		Cannon		Kojak	
	NBC	Local		Chase	NBC Wednesday Mystery Movie			Love Story	
THURSDAY	ABC	Local		Toma		Kung Fu		The Streets of San Francisco	
	CBS	Local		The Waltons		The CBS Thursday Night Movie			
	NBC	Local		The Flip Wilson Show		Ironside		The Dean Martin Show	
FRIDAY	ABC	Local		The Brady Bunch	The Odd Couple	Room 222	Adam's Rib	Love American Style	
	CBS	Local		Dirty Sally	Good Times	The CBS Friday Night Movies			
	NBC	Local		Sanford & Son	Lotsa Luck	The Girl with Something Extra	The Brian Keith Show	The Dean Martin Comedy Hour	

TOP RATED TV SHOWS
(1973-1974 Season)

All in the Family
The Waltons
Sanford and Son
M*A*S*H
Hawaii Five-0
Maude
Kojak
Sonny & Cher Hour
The Mary Tyler Moore Show
Cannon
Bob Newhart Show

Betty White makes her first appearance as Sue Ann Nivens on the *Mary Tyler Moore Show* 4th season opener, and Sherman Hemsley appears for the first time as George Jefferson on *All in the Family*.

Betty White & Sherman Hemsley

Best Dramatic Series
The Waltons

Best Comedy Series
All in the Family

Best Variety Series
The Julie Andrews Hour

Best Drama Series Actor
Richard Thomas *The Waltons*

Best Drama Series Actress
Michael Learned *The Waltons*

Best Comedy Series Actor
Jack Klugman *The Odd Couple*

Best Comedy Series Actress
Mary Tyler Moore
Mary Tyler Moore Show

Cast of All in the Family: *Carrol O'Connor, Jean Stapleton, Rob Reiner, Sally Struthers*

BORN IN 1973

TYRA BANKS ★ TEMPESTT BLEDSOE ★ CARSON DALY ★ OMAR EPPS ★ VERA FARMIGA ★ BRIAN AUSTIN GREEN ★ MARIO LOPEZ ★ RACHEL MADDOW ★ SETH MYERS ★ TORI SPELLING

Mario Lopez

DIED IN 1973

JOHN BANNER, 63 *HOGAN'S HEROES* ACTOR ★ IRENE RYAN, 70 *BEVERLY HILLBILLIES* ACTRESS

Irene Ryan

BE ON THE LOOKOUT FOR CAPTAIN JOHN.... AND YOUR CHANCE TO GRAB A KHJ BEACH TOWEL IN THE SUMMER OF 93!

NEW MUSIC

LET'S GET IT ON	Marvin Gaye
I BELIEVE IN YOU	Johnnie Taylor
A MILLION TO ONE	Donny Osmond

LOS ANGELES' FAVORITE ALBUMS

Last Week	This Week	Title	Artist	Weeks
(2)	1.	HOUSES OF THE HOLY	Led Zeppelin	15
(1)	2.	LIVING IN THE MATERIAL WORLD	George Harrison	6
(5)	3.	MADE IN JAPAN	Deep Purple	5
(6)	4.	NOW AND THEN	Carpenters	7
(3)	5.	RED ROSE SPEEDWAY	Paul McCartney & Wings	10
(4)	6.	DARK SIDE OF THE MOON	Pink Floyd	15
(9)	7.	BILLION DOLLAR BABIES	Alice Cooper	18
(8)	8.	DIAMOND GIRL	Seals & Crofts	13
(10)	9.	FANTASY	Carole King	5
(7)	10.	THERE GOES RHYMIN' SIMON	Paul Simon	8
(22)	11.	CHICAGO VI	Chicago	2
(12)	12.	DON'T SHOOT ME I'M ONLY THE PIANO PLAYER	Elton John	24
(19)	13.	LEON LIVE	Leon Russell	3
(13)	14.	THE CAPTAIN AND ME	The Doobie Brothers	12
(11)	15.	THE BEST OF BREAD	Bread	16
(16)	16.	NATURAL HIGH	Bloodstone	4
(17)	17.	YESSONGS	Yes	8
(15)	18.	THEY ONLY COME OUT AT NIGHT	The Edgar Winter Group	18
(18)	19.	TALKING BOOK	Stevie Wonder	31
(14)	20.	THE BEATLES / 1967-1970	The Beatles	13
(21)	21.	TOWER OF POWER	Tower of Power	3
(26)	22.	FRESH	Sly & The Family Stone	3
(25)	23.	HOT AUGUST NIGHT	Neil Diamond	32
(24)	24.	RECORDED LIVE	Ten Years After	3
(20)	25.	THE BEATLES / 1962-1966	The Beatles	13
(22)	26.	CALL ME	Al Green	10
(—)	27.	MACHINE HEAD	Deep Purple	1
(28)	28.	BLOODSHOT	J. Geils Band	5
(30)	29.	MASTERPIECE	Temptations	18
(29)	30.	NO SECRETS	Carly Simon	31

93 KHJ 'THIRTY'

JULY 12, 1973

Last Week	This Week	Title	Artist	Weeks
(1)	1.	ONE TIN SOLDIER	Coven	6
(7)	2.	MONSTER MASH	Bobby (Boris) Pickett & The Crypt-Kickers	6
(2)	3.	NATURAL HIGH	Bloodstone	8
(4)	4.	SHAMBALA	Three Dog Night	8
(3)	5.	SMOKE ON THE WATER	Deep Purple	7
(5)	6.	YESTERDAY ONCE MORE	Carpenters	6
(9)	7.	BAD, BAD LEROY BROWN	Jim Croce	6
(12)	8.	LIVE AND LET DIE	Paul McCartney & Wings	4
(10)	9.	BOOGIE WOOGIE BUGLE BOY	Bette Midler	4
(14)	10.	SO VERY HARD TO GO	Tower of Power	4
(11)	11.	THE MORNING AFTER	Maureen McGovern	5
(25)	12.	BROTHER LOUIE	Stories	2
(13)	13.	GET DOWN	Gilbert O'Sullivan	6
(17)	14.	BEHIND CLOSED DOORS	Charlie Rich	3
(16)	15.	DADDY COULD SWEAR, I DECLARE	Gladys Knight & The Pips	5
(6)	16.	GIVE ME LOVE (GIVE ME PEACE ON EARTH)	George Harrison	10
(21)	17.	YOUNG LOVE	Donny Osmond	3
(20)	18.	TIME TO GET DOWN	KH O'Jays	4
(24)	19.	SAY, HAS ANYBODY SEEN MY SWEET GYPSY ROSE	Dawn	3
(8)	20.	WILL IT GO ROUND IN CIRCLES	Billy Preston	8
(15)	21.	KODACHROME	Paul Simon	9
(29)	22.	UNEASY RIDER	Charlie Daniels	2
(—)	23.	TOUCH ME IN THE MORNING	Diana Ross	1
(27)	24.	DIAMOND GIRL	Seals & Crofts	2
(22)	25.	PILLOW TALK	Sylvia	12
(—)	26.	LET'S GET IT ON	Marvin Gaye	1
(30)	27.	FEELIN' STRONGER EVERY DAY	Chicago	2
(—)	28.	I BELIEVE IN YOU	Johnnie Taylor	1
(19)	29.	ONE OF A KIND (Love Affair)	Spinners	7
(18)	30.	PLAYGROUND IN MY MIND	Clint Holmes	13

1973 ADVERTISEMENT

Popular Music

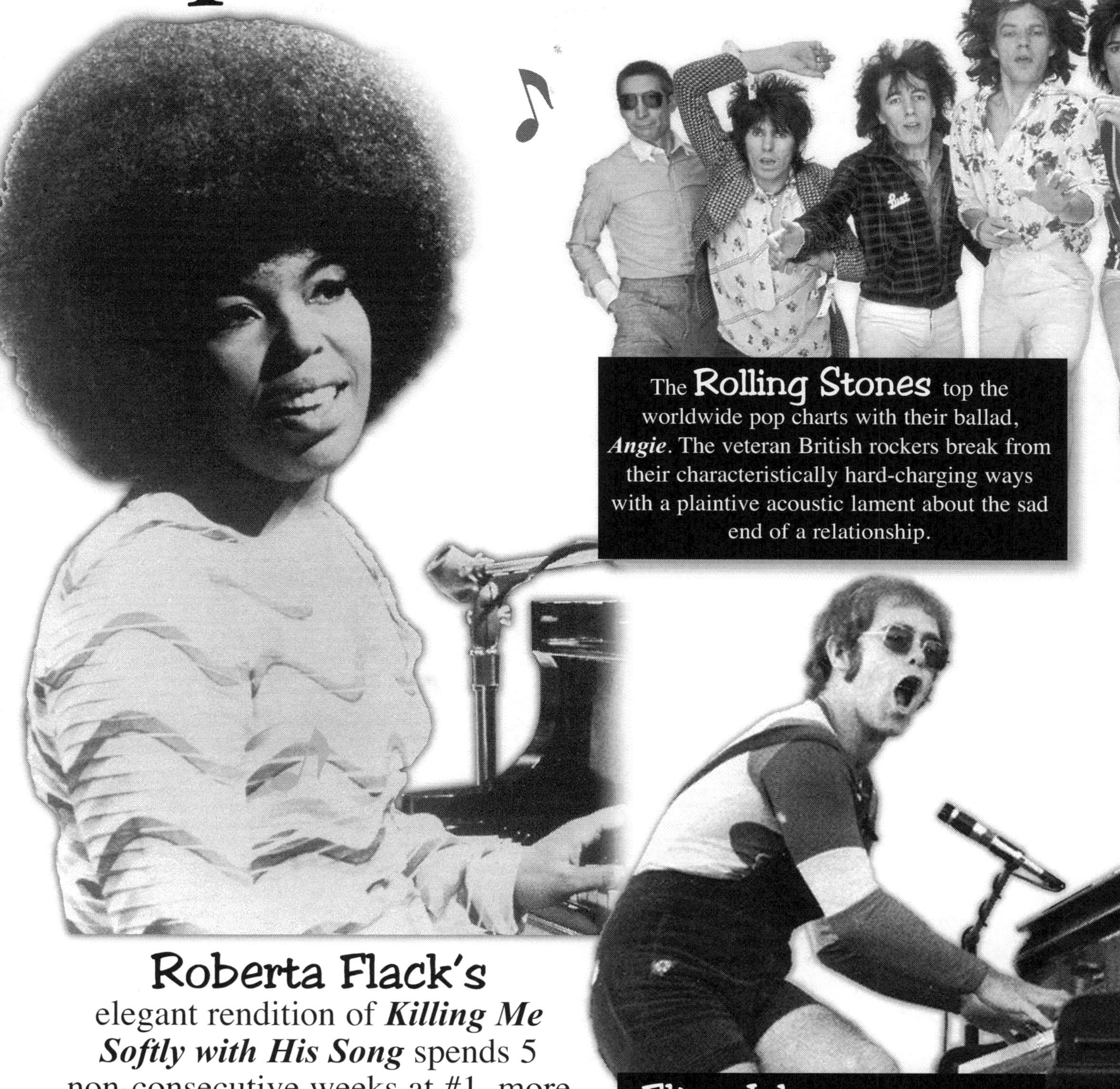

The **Rolling Stones** top the worldwide pop charts with their ballad, ***Angie***. The veteran British rockers break from their characteristically hard-charging ways with a plaintive acoustic lament about the sad end of a relationship.

Roberta Flack's elegant rendition of ***Killing Me Softly with His Song*** spends 5 non-consecutive weeks at #1, more than any other single in 1973. Her recording wins the Grammy for Record of the Year and Best Female Pop Vocal Performance.

Elton John scores his first U.S. #1 hit single with, ***Crocodile Rock***, a rowdy number loaded with nostalgia for youthful rebellion and the early days of Rock and Roll.

1973 POPULAR SONGS BY CHART POSITION

Angie	Rolling Stones
Tie a Yellow Ribbon 'Round The Old Oak Tree	Tony Orlando & Dawn
Killing Me Softly with His Song	Roberta Flack
You're So Vain	Carly Simon
Crocodile Rock	Elton John
I'd Love You to Want Me	Lobo
Tha Ballroom Blitz	The Sweet
Goodbye Yellow Brick Road	Elton John
Superstition	Stevie Wonder
Get Down	Gilbert O'Sullivan
Photograph	Ringo Starr
Top of the World	Carpenters
Daniel	Elton John
You Are the Sunshine of My Life	Stevie Wonder
Can the Can	Suzi Quatro
Blockbuster	The Sweet
Smoke on the Water	Deep Purple
Let's Get it On	Marvin Gaye
Space Oddity	David Bowie
Yesterday Once More	Carpenters
The Morning After	Maureen McGovern
My Love	Wings
Brother Louie	Stories
Walk on the Wild Side	Lou Reed
Stuck in the Middle with You	Stealer's Wheel
Me & Mrs. Jones	Billy Paul
Live & Let Die	Wings
Why Can't We Live Together?	Timmy Thomas
Midnight Train to Georgia	Gladys Knight/Pips
Delta Dawn	Helen Reddy
Bad, Bad Leroy Brown	Jim Croce
Love Train	The O'Jays
Long Train Runnin'	Doobie Brothers
Frankenstein	Edgar Winter
48 Crash	Suzi Quatro
Money	Pink Floyd
Nutbush City Limits	Ike & Tina Turner
Superfly	Curtis Mayfield
Cisco Kid	War
Half-breed	Cher
Give Me Love	George Harrison
Kodachrome	Paul Simon
Shambala	Three Dog Night

Stevie Wonder
Carly Simon
The Carpenters
Marvin Gaye

The 16th Annual Grammy Awards recognize accomplishments from 1973

Bette Midler

Charlie Rich

song of the year
Killing Me Softly with His Song
Roberta Flack (performer) • Fox & Gimbel (songwriters)

record of the year
Killing Me Softly with His Song
Roberta Flack & Joel Dorn (producer)

album of the year
Innervisions
Stevie Wonder (producer/artist)

new artist
Bette Midler

male pop vocal performance
You Are the Sunshine of My Life
Stevie Wonder

female pop vocal performance
Killing Me Softly with His Song
Roberta Flack

rhythm & blues song
Superstition Stevie Wonder (performer, songwriter)

country + western song
Behind Closed Doors
Charlie Rich (performer) • Kenny O'Dell (songwriter)

new bands

AC/DC
Bad Company
Devo
Journey
Kansas
Kiss
Los Lobos
Quiet Riot

1973

LEONARD COHEN: LIVE SONGS

SIDE ONE:
1. Minute Prologue
London 1972
2. Passing Thru
London 1972
3. You Know Who I Am
Brussels 1972
4. Bird on the Wire
Paris 1972
5. Nancy
London 1972
6. Improvisation
Paris 1972

SIDE TWO:
1. Story of Isaac
Berlin 1972
2. Please Don't Pass Me By
(A Disgrace)
London 1970
3. Tonight Will Be Fine
Isle of Wight 1970
4. Queen Victoria
Room in Tennessee 1972

Produced by Bob Johnston
Bob Potter: Engineer
All songs
Stranger Music Inc.(BMI)
Cover photograph by S.B Elrod

MUSICIANS 1972
Ron Cornelius
Acoustic and Electric Guitar
Peter Marshal
Stand-up and Electric Bass
David O'Connor
Acoustic Guitar
Bob Johnston
Organ
Leonard Cohen
Acoustic Guitar
Donna Washburn
Vocals
Jennifer Warren
Vocals

MUSICIANS 1970
Ron Cornelius
Electric Guitar
Charlie Daniels
Electric Bass
and Fiddle
Elkin Fowler
Banjo and Guitar
Bob Johnston
Harmonica and Guitar
Leonard Cohen
Acoustic Guitar
Aileen Fowler
Vocals
Corlynn Hanney
Vocals

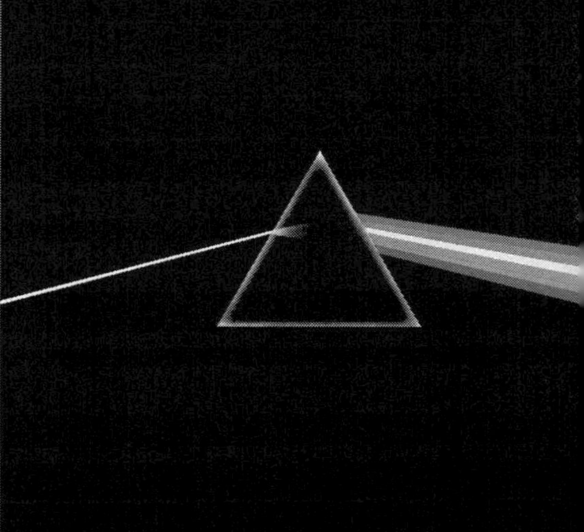

RECORD COLLECTION

Pink Floyd

The late night musical variety series *The Midnight Special* debuts on TV, as does a similar after hours program, *Don Kirshner's Rock Concert*. Both shows enjoy a nearly decade-long run, each featuring top names in pop, rock and R&B, including **AC/DC**, **ARETHA FRANKLIN**, **DAVID BOWIE**, **RAY CHARLES**, **The JACKSON FIVE**, **TOM PETTY and the HEARTBREAKERS**, **FLEETWOOD MAC**, **MARVIN GAYE**, **LINDA RONSTADT**, **VAN MORRISON**, **ROD STEWART**, and many others.

PINK FLOYD releases *Dark Side of the Moon*. The LP stays on the *Billboard* charts for a record-smashing 741 weeks. In May, **LED ZEPPELIN** embarks on a U.S. tour. They set concert attendance records, topping numbers previously held by The Beatles. A show at Tampa Stadium in Florida logs 56,800 attendees. **THE WHO** also launch a highly successful tour in support of their acclaimed album, *Quadrophenia*.

The Who

In front of 3,500 fans at a July London concert, **DAVID BOWIE** announces that he is retiring his Ziggy Stardust alter ego.

David Bowie

JAZZ AND BLUES Passings 1973

Blues singer, guitarist and songwriter **Memphis Minnie** (76) recorded about 200 songs, including "When the Levee Breaks."

Jazz tenor saxophonist **Ben Webster** (65) was a soloist with the Duke Ellington Orchestra before launching his solo career, recording extensively as a leader & sideman.

Memphis Minnie

Ben Webster

Gene Krupa

Willie "The Lion" Smith (79) gained renown for developing the stride piano style, with it's roots in jazz, blues & ragtime.

Flamboyant drummer and bandleader **Gene Krupa** (64) will be remembered, among other things, for his drum solo on Benny Goodman's 1937 recording of "Sing, Sing, Sing."

DIED IN 1973

Popular "Dream Lover" and "Mack the Knife" singer **Bobby Darin** (37) passes away from heart ailments on December 20th.

"Bad, Bad Leroy Brown" singer/songwriter **Jim Croce** (30) dies in a Louisiana chartered plane crash on September 20th.

Gram Parsons (26), known for his work with the Byrds & the Flying Burrito Brothers, dies of a drug overdose, September 19th.

Grateful Dead founding member **Ron "Pigpen" McKernan** (27) dies from gastrointestinal hemorrhage spurred by alcoholism on March 8th.

BORN IN 1973

★ FAITH EVANS ★ FLESH-N-BONE ★ SAVION GLOVER ★ KRAYZIE BONE ★ NICK LACHEY ★ MOS DEF ★ NAS ★ SHANICE ★ RUFUS WAINWRIGHT ★ PHARRELL WILLIAMS ★ GRETCHEN WILSON

Pharrell Williams

Electric jazz and jazz fusion continue to be dominant forces in 1973 improvisation-based recorded music. A fusion classic, **Mahavishnu Orchestra's *Birds of Fire*** LP ranges from soaring to contemplative, driven by the stinging electric guitar of bandleader **John McGlaughlin**. Latin jazz makes it's presence felt in the skyrocket tenor sax solos of **Gato Barbieri** on ***Chapter One: Latin America***, and in the power scatting of Brazilian singer **Flora Purim** in ***Butterfly Dreams***. Pianist **Herbie Hancock** goes solid funk-fusion with the LP ***Headhunters***, while **McCoy Tyner** releases ***Enlightenment***, a gorgeous and dynamic live album from the Montreux Jazz Festival.

Herbie Hancock

Flora Purim

1973 ADVERTISEMENT

BIG HOLIDAY SPECIAL

CIVIC AUDITORIUM

227 LYON ST., N. W.--GRAND RAPIDS, MICH.

SAT. DEC. 29 8:30 P. M.

ADVANCE ADMISSION $6.50--AT DOOR $7.50

THE GODFATHER OF SOUL...IN CONCERT

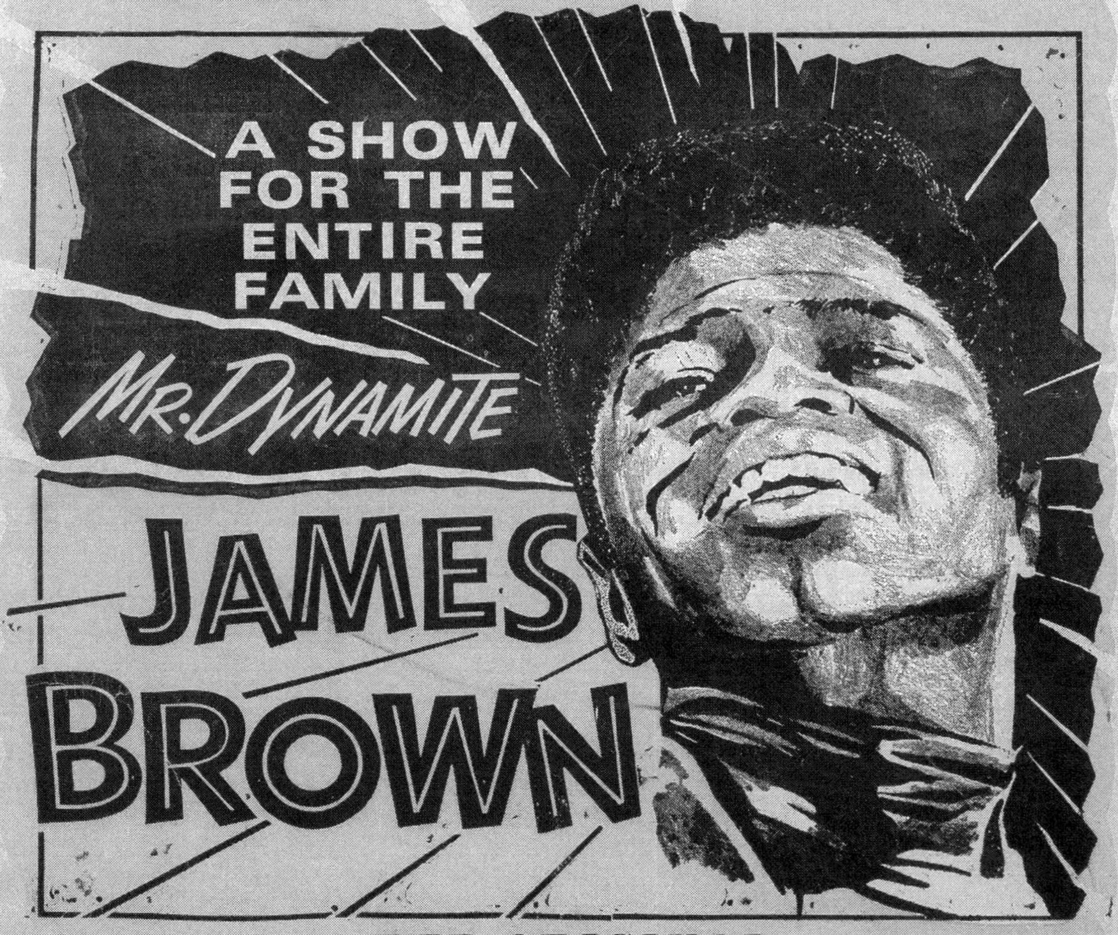

THE ORIGINAL

DISCO MAN

"PLEASE, PLEASE" ★ "BODY HEAT" ★ "MAN'S WORLD"
"THAT WAS THE TIME" ★ "TRY ME"

The J. B.'s MARTHA HYATT

COUNTRY & WESTERN #1 HITS

Soul Song	Joe Stampley
(Old Dogs, Children and) Watermelon Wine	Tom T. Hall
I Wonder if They Ever Think of Me	Merle Haggard
Rated "X"	Loretta Lynn
'Til I Get it Right	Tammy Wynette
A Shoulder to Cry On	Charley Pride
Come Live With Me	Roy Clark
What's Your Mama's Name	Tanya Tucker
Why Me	Kris Kristofferson
Trip to Heaven	Freddie Hart
You Were Always There	Donna Fargo

Patsy Cline

Patsy Cline (1932-1963) is the first female to be inducted into the Country Music Hall of Fame as a solo act. **Chet Atkins** (1924-2001) is inducted as well.

Left to right: Loretta Lynn, Merle Haggard, Tammy Wynette, Charley Pride

Country Music Association Awards

ENTERTAINER OF THE YEAR: **Roy Clark** / TOP MALE VOCALIST: **Charlie Rich** / TOP FEMALE VOCALIST: **Loretta Lynn** / TOP VOCAL DUO: **Conway Twitty & Loretta Lynn** / SINGLE OF THE YEAR: ***Behind Closed Doors*** **– Charlie Rich** / SONG OF THE YEAR: ***Behind Closed Doors*** **– Charlie Rich** / INSTRUMENTALIST OF THE YEAR: **Charlie McCoy**

Willie Nelson stages his first annual 4th of July Picnic in Dripping Springs, TX. 40,000 fans are entertained by Willie along with many guest artists.

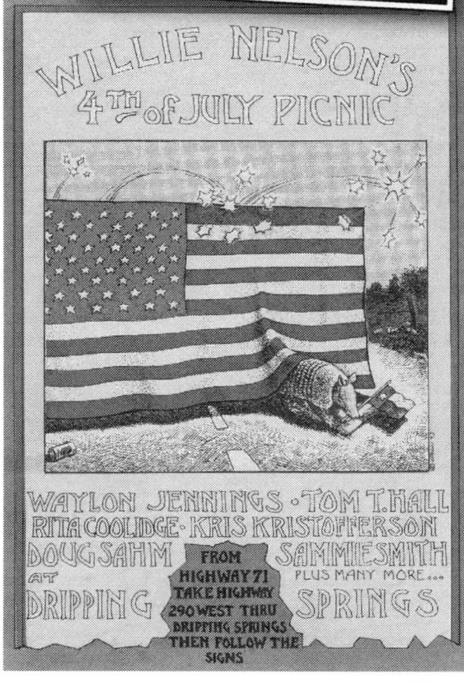

1973 ADVERTISEMENT

'73 CORVETTE

We gave it radials, a quieter ride, guard beams and a nose job.

Like every new generation of Corvettes, this one has its own distinct appeal.

But it also has some very distinct advantages.

Standard GR70-15 steel-belted radial ply tires, for example. And interior compartment sound levels that have been reduced by 40%. Plus the security of steel guard beams in the doors.

But what everybody notices first is the aerodynamic front end that's formed to follow a variety of functions. First of all, it protects. The body-color front bumper is stronger. It's specially mounted and has an outer cover made of injection-molded urethane to resist dents and prevent rust.

The new domed hood is special, too. Its air-induction design improves high output engine operation.

The swooping shape of the front end even takes care of covering the headlights and the windshield wipers.

Because with a car like the '73 Vette, it's hard to say where function ends and where form begins.

And that's precisely the beauty of it all.

Building a better way to see the U.S.A. Chevrolet

GM
MARK OF EXCELLENCE

Classical Music

Bernstein

Stern

For the first time,
Leonard Bernstein
conducts Tchaikovsky's
Violin Concerto, with the
New York Philharmonic.
Isaac Stern
is the soloist.

English composer
Benjamin Britten
debuts his opera, *Death in Venice* at Britain's annual Aldeburgh Festival. The two-act composition is based on novelist Thomas Mann's novella of the same name.

Steve Reich's
composition, *Music for Mallet Instruments, Voices and Organ,* utilizes glockenspiels, marimbas and women's voices.

New Works

Symphony No. 10
Eduard Tubin

Six Poems for Marina Tsvetaeva, Po. 143
Dmitri Shostakovich

Makrokosmos, Vol. II for amplified piano
George Crumb

Etcetera for small orchestra, tape and three conductors
John Cage

Fantasy Sonata for flute and harp
William Alwyn

Paisajes Mexicano for orchestra
Carlos Chavez

For FrankO'Hara for flute, clarinet, percussion, piano, violin & cello
Morton Feldman

Music on Open Strings (Symphony No. 1)
Gloria Coates

Nocturne
Akira Miyoshi

De Temporum Fine Comoedia
Carl Orff

Symphony No. 7
Malcolm Arnold

Pulitzer Prize

String Quartet No. 3
Elliott Carter

The Metropolitan Opera produces a special issue of *Opera News* to celebrate the 100th anniversary of fabled tenor **ENRICO CARUSO's** birth.

PASSINGS

Pablo Casals (b. 1876) dies of a heart attack at the age of 96. Regarded as one of the finest cellists of all time, the Catalonia-born virtuoso is especially remembered for his recordings of the Bach Cello Suites and was awarded the Presidential Medal of Freedom by John F. Kennedy in 1963.

Conductor **Otto Klemperer** (b. 1885) passes away at the age of 88. He fled Nazi Germany for the U.S. in the '30s, and was appointed music director of the Los Angeles Philharmonic. In 1959, he became conductor of London's Philharmonia Orchestra, producing numerous memorable recordings.

Casals

Britain's **Queen Elizabeth** travels to Australia in October to open the new **Sydney Opera House**. The televised launch includes fireworks and a performance of Beethoven's ***Symphony No. 9***.

Virtuoso **Jascha Heifetz** deposits parts of his Guarnerius violin in the concrete foundation of the Virginia Ramo Hall of Music at USC in order to ensure that the new building is "in tune."

The Metropolitan Opera's production of *The Magic Flute* marks the debut of American soprano **Benita Valente**.

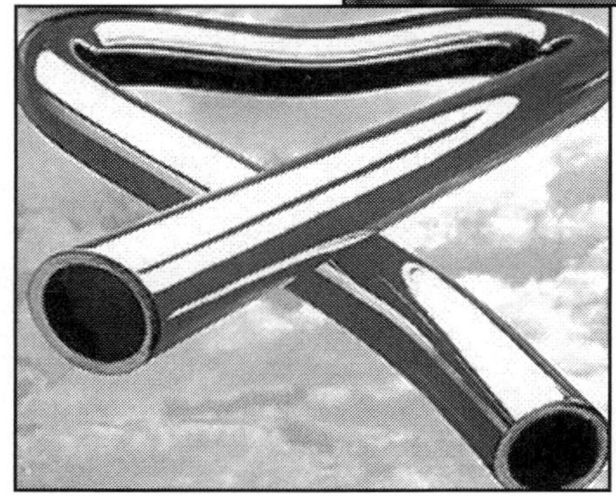

Mike Oldfield's hit instrumental solo work, *Tubular Bells*, is the first release of Richard Branson's Virgin Records.

Classical GRAMMYS

Best Classical Performance - Orchestra
Pierre Boulez (conductor) & the New York Philharmonic for Bartók: *Concerto for Orchestra*

Best Classical Vocal Soloist
Leontyne Price & the New Philharmonia Orchestra for Puccini: *Heroines*

Best Opera Recording
Tom Mowrey (producer), Leonard Bernstein (conductor), Marilyn Horne, Tom Krause, Adriana Maliponte, James McCracken & the Metropolitan Opera Orchestra & Chorus for Bizet: *Carmen*

Classical Album of the Year
Thomas Z. Shepard (producer), Pierre Boulez (conductor) & the New York Philharmonic for Bartók: *Concerto for Orchestra*

Best Chamber Performance
Gunther Schuller (conductor) & the New England Conservatory Ragtime Ensemble for Joplin: *The Red Back Book*

1973 ADVERTISEMENT

the dance company
(N.S.W.)

in the
SYDNEY
OPERA HOUSE

A spectacular
Australian first
for dance.
An open public season.
The Concert Hall
November 2-10 1973.

Australia's
own contemporary
dance company
in association with
the Sydney
Opera House Trust
presenting three
distinguished
world premières.

ON BROADWAY

~ Plummer's Year ~

Actor Christopher Plummer lands the Tony and Drama Desk awards for his work in the title role of Cyrano, at Broadway's Palace Theatre. The novelist Anthony Burgess penned the lyrics for the musical, based on the 1897 play about a love~struck 17th~century duelist with an extravagant nose.

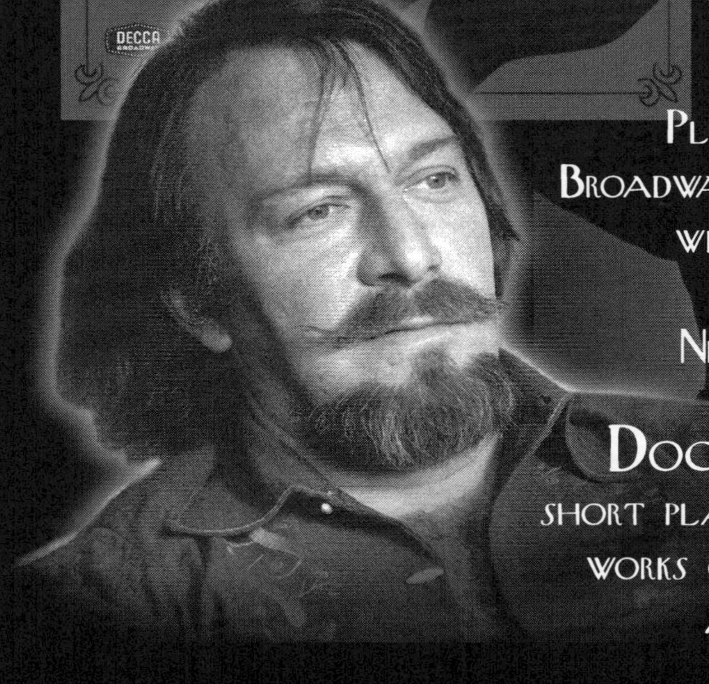

Plummer's bountiful Broadway year continues with a role in the award~winning Neil Simon comedy, The Good Doctor, a series of short plays based on the works of Russian writer Anton Chekhov.

ANOTHER OPENING, ANOTHER NIGHT

Cast of *A Little Night Music*

SEESAW

THE RIVER NIGER

A LITTLE NIGHT MUSIC

SONDHEIM: A MUSICAL TRIBUTE

THE WOMEN

THE PAJAMA GAME

THE ICEMAN COMETH

UNCLE VANYA

Raisin Rises!

Debbie Allen, Virginia Capers and Joe Morton are among the cast members of Raisin, a musical based on Lorraine Hansberry's play, A Raisin in the Sun. The inspiring hit has an 847 performance run, snagging 9 Tony nominations with 2 wins, and the soundtrack album goes on to win a Grammy Award.

RAISIN

1973's biggest broadway bomb

***Rachel Lily Rosenbloom** (and Don't You Ever Forget It)*

Originally written for Bette Midler — who turned the part down — the musical flop about a Hollywood gossip columnist closes during December previews, only a few days after opening.

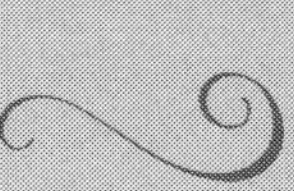

Tony Awards

28th Annual Tony Awards held on April 21, 1974 for 1973 productions

BEST PLAY
"The River Niger"
Joseph A Walker (playwright)

BEST MUSICAL
"Raisin"
Robert Nemiroff (producer)

BEST ACTOR in a PLAY
Michael Moriarty
"Find Your Way Home"

BEST ACTRESS in a PLAY
Colleen Dewhurst
"A Moon for the Misbegotten"

BEST DIRECTOR - PLAY
José Quintero
"A Moon for the Misbegotten"

BEST ACTOR in a MUSICAL
Christopher Plummer
"Cyrano"

BEST ACTRESS in a MUSICAL
Virginia Capers
"Raisin"

BEST DIRECTOR - MUSICAL
Harold Prince
"Candide"

BEST CHOREOGRAPHY
Michael Bennett
"Seesaw"

PULITZER PRIZE for DRAMA
JASON MILLER (writer)
"That Championship Season"

THAT CHAMPIONSHIP SEASON

What Else Is Playing:

Look Away

☆

Tricks

☆

The Enemy Is Dead

☆

Don Juan in Hell

☆

The Jockey Club Stakes

☆

Medea

☆

The Changing Room

☆

No Sex Please, We're British

☆

The Merchant of Venice

☆

No Hard Feelings

☆

The Play's the Thing

☆

A Streetcar Named Desire

☆

Boom Boom Room

DON JUAN IN HELL

Colleen Dewhurst & Jason Robards in A Moon for the Misbegotten

GiGi

What Else Is Playing:

The Waltz of the Toreadors

☆

Gigi

☆

Chemin de Fer

☆

The Three Sisters

☆

The Beggar's Opera

☆

Children of the Wind

☆

Veronica's Room

☆

A Moon for the Misbegotten

☆

Measure for Measure

☆

The Visit

☆

The Plough and the Stars

☆

Bette Midler

☆

Let Me Hear You Smile

The Motorola Car Entertainment Center gets it all together

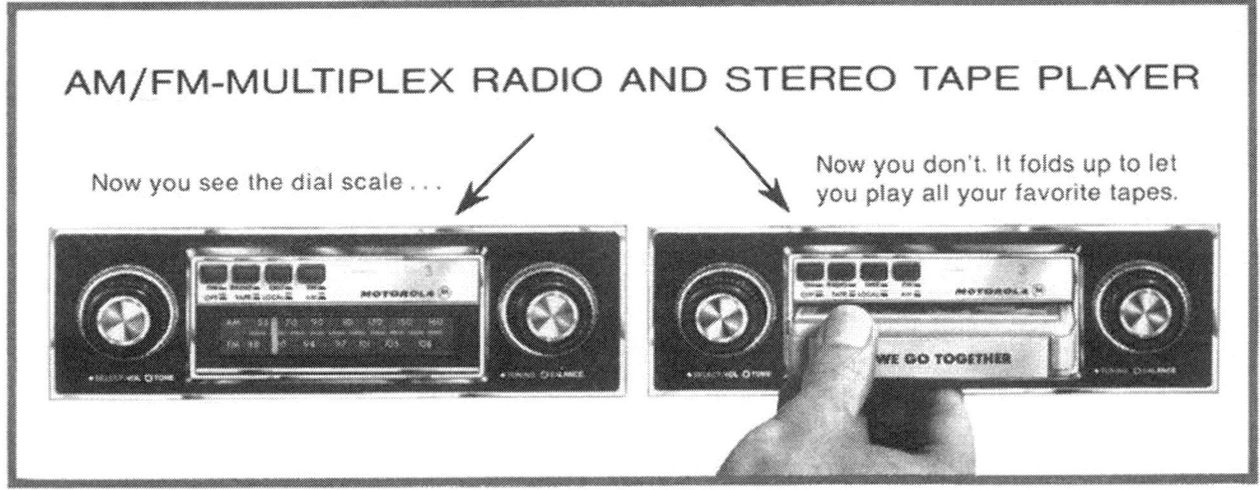

It's all in one, all in the dash!

Now Motorola stashes it all in the dash—puts a precision-built, compact solid-state Entertainment Center in one handy unit.

Enjoy the now sounds on the AM band. Get the full stereo treatment of FM-Multiplex—two discrete channels that surround you with music. All this and a stereo tape player, too.

Made to fit the dash of a wide variety of cars. Tomorrow's Car Entertainment Center . . . here today at your nearest Motorola Dealer.

Model TF852AX. Local/Distance Switch FM Control for clear listening signal, Push Pull Audio Output, Dual Tone Control, Balance Control, Dual Volume Control, Stereo Indicator, 14 Tuned Circuits, Speakers optional extra.

A Legend Passes

1907 self portrait

April 8, 1973 — Spanish artist **Pablo Picasso** dies of heart failure at his home in Mougins, France at the age of 91. Probably the most influential artist of the 20th century, his voluminous body of work is often categorized into periods, from the early Blue and Rose periods, to the experimental Cubist and neoclassical works. His prolific genius found expression in painting, sculpture, prints, ceramics, murals and theatrical designs. Along the way, he accrued international acclaim and a substantial fortune.

Art Thievery

On December 18th, two burglars with guns tie up a night watchman at Cincinnati's Taft Museum and make off with a pair of Rembrandt paintings – "Man Leaning on a Sill" and "Portrait of an Elderly Woman." A couple of days later, the thieves make known their ransom price of $300,000, threatening to burn the paintings if their demand is not met. Brokered by a former TV news host, the exchange is covered on live local TV. A few days later, police arrest three men and recover the money.

Decades later, art experts determine that the stolen Rembrandts were never authentic, but copies made by the artists' students. The Museum no longer displays the art.

Man Leaning on a Sill

DUBUFFET
THE GUGGENHEIM MUSEUM
APRIL 27
JULY 29
1973

Artist **Alexander Calder**, renowned for his kinetic mobile sculptures, paints a Braniff DC-8-62 airliner as a flying canvas.

1973 Art Highlights

Andy Warhol – *Mao*, silkscreen & acrylic

Barbara Hepworth – *Conversation with Magic Stones*, sculpture

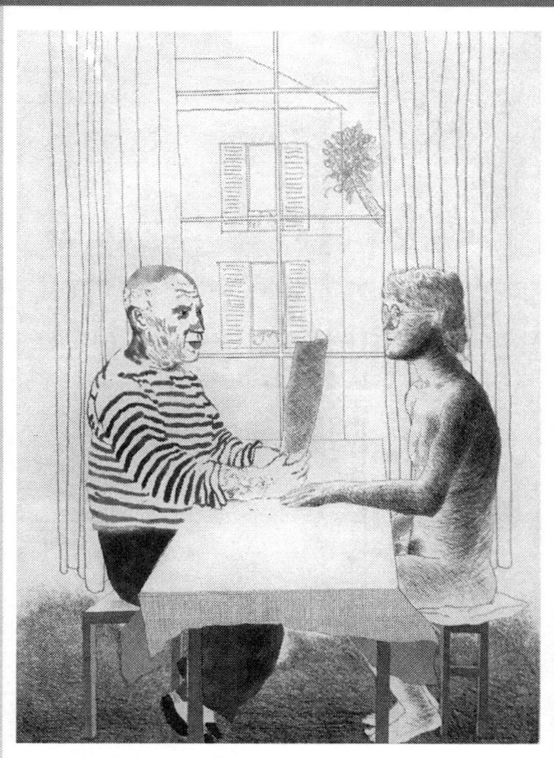

David Hockney – *Artist and Model*, etching

The **Van Gogh Museum** opens in Amsterdam's Museum Square near the Stedelijk Museum and the Rijksmuseum. Dedicated to the Dutch artist Vincent van Gogh and his contemporaries, the museum boasts the world's largest collection of his work.

Self portrait detail

BORN IN 1973 ★ The mysterious graffiti artist BANKSY may or may not have been born on July 28th.

PASSINGS

Edward Steichen, Marlene Dietrich, *1934*

Highly regarded photographer **Edward Steichen** (93), is credited with elevating photography to an artform with his sumptuous pictorial and portrait images.

American artist **Robert Smithson** dies in a light plane crash at the age of 35. Smithson was one of the artists who pioneered "earthworks"— art installations often sited in remote locations utilizing organic materials. Smithson's "Spiral Jetty" is a 1,500 foot long coil constructed of rock and salt, jutting into Great Salt Lake.

Robert Smithson, Spiral Jetty, *1969-70*

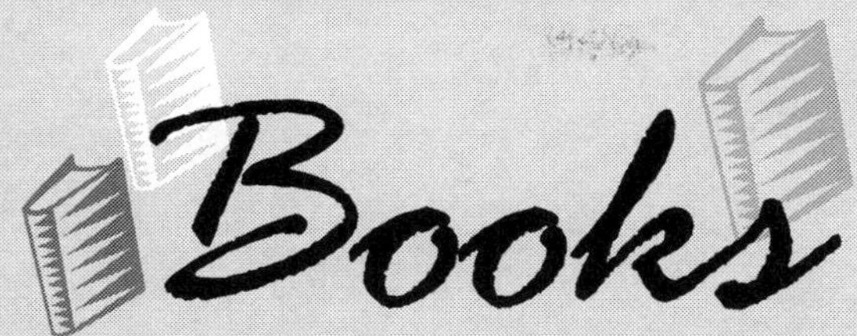

Books

ART MEETS POLITICS

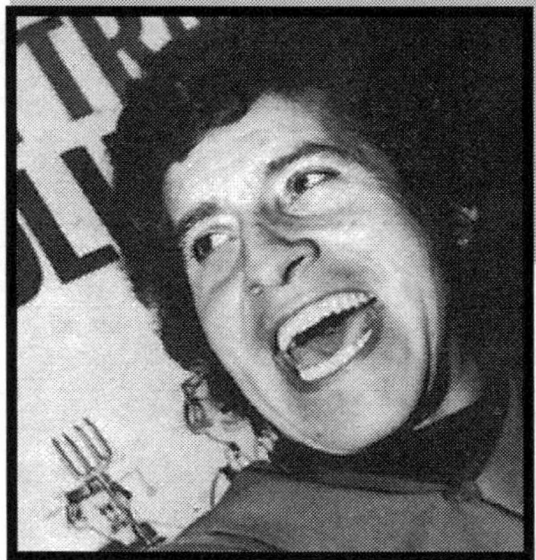

Chilean poet and theater director **Victor Jara** developed Chilean theater by producing and directing local works and classics, as well as promoting new Chilean music. Shortly after the Chilean coup of September 1973, which overthrew Salvador Allende and installed the right wing dictator Augusto Pinochet, Jara is arrested for his political activism. Tortured and ultimately killed, his body is thrown out on the street of a Santiago shantytown. A final poem, hidden inside the shoe of a friend, survives Jara.

Following the 1973 publication of ***The Gulag Archipelago***, dissident novelist **Aleksandr Solzhenitsyn's** 3-volume exposé of the Soviet forced labor camp system, he is arrested for treason. Eventually expelled from the Soviet Union in 1974, he is barred from returning for twenty years. The recipient of a 1970 Nobel Prize in Literature, Solzhenitsyn's works have been widely translated and *Gulag* becomes quickly available in English and French.

PASSINGS

Pearl S. Buck (80)	**Pablo Neruda** (69)
J. R. R. Tolkien (81)	**W. H. Auden** (66)

NOBEL PRIZE FOR LITERATURE

Patrick White

Australia

PULITZER PRIZE

Eudora Welty

FICTION

The Optimist's Daughter

Eudora Welty

POETRY

Up Country

Maxine Kumin

BOOKER PRIZE

The Siege of Krishnapur

J. G. Farrell

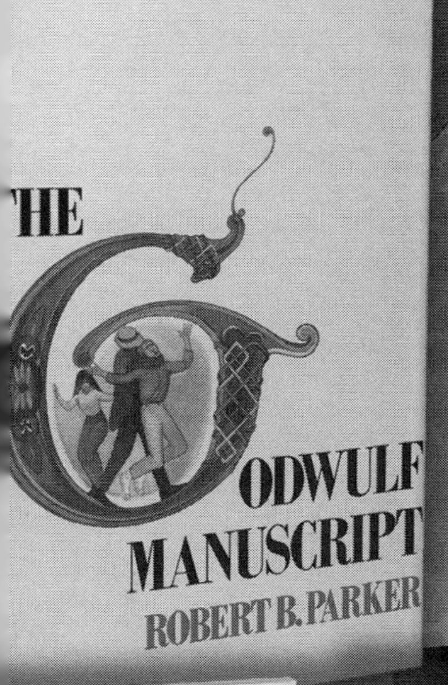
THE
GODWULF
MANUSCRIPT
ROBERT B. PARKER

J.G. BALLARD
CRASH

MOMO
A Novel by
MICHAEL ENDE
Author of
THE NEVERENDING STORY
DEAN
KOONTZ
Demon Seed

Child
of
God
A NOVEL BY
CORMAC
McCARTHY
Author of The Orchard Keeper and Outer Dark
THE
DEVIL TREE
Jerzy Kosinski
TIME
ENOUGH
FOR LOVE
ROBERT A.
HEINLEIN
Graham Greene
The Honorary Consul
Graham
Greene
The
Honorary
Consul
A Novel

ANTHONY POWELL
TEMPORARY KINGS

The Black Prince
IRIS MURDOCH
The Black Prince
IRIS MURDOCH
VLADIMIR
NABOKOV
TRANSPARENT
THINGS
A New Novel
by the
Author of LOLITA
and ADA
A New
Novel By
Jacquelin
Susann
Once
Is Not
Enough

SERPICO
The cop who defied the system
PETER MAAS
Author of THE VALACHI PAPERS
A Novel
BURR
GORE VIDAL

NELSON ALGREN
Author of MAN WITH THE GOLDEN ARM
THE LAST CAROUSEL

THE RACHEL PAPERS
MARTIN AMIS

SOLZHENITSYN
The Gulag Archipelago
SULA
A novel by TONI MORRISON

ROBERT LUDLUM
Author of THE SCARLATTI INHERITANCE and THE OSTERMAN WEEKEND
THE MATLOCK PAPER
A NOVEL
JEAN POIRET
Théâtre 1
La Cage aux folles
suivi de Douce-amère

Kurt Vonnegut, Jr.
BREAKFAST OF CHAMPIONS
A NOVEL
FEAR AND LOATHING: ON THE CAMPAIGN TRAIL '72
Dr. Hunter S. Thompson
with Illustrations by Ralph Steadman

The Princess Bride
S. Morgenstern's Classic Tale of True Love and High Adventure
The 'good parts' version
Abridged by
WILLIAM GOLDMAN
Author of Butch Cassidy and the Sundance Kid

SYBI

architecture

reach for the sky

New skyscrapers vie for the title, *Tallest Building in the World.*

The Twin Towers of New York's **World Trade Center** are the world's tallest buildings at the time of their 1973 opening, topping at 1,368 feet. They are tragically decimated in the September 11, 2001 terror attacks.

When completed in 1973, Chicago's **Sears Tower** surpasses the World Trade Center at 1,450 feet, becoming the world's tallest building for the next 25 years.

and design

One of the most iconic structures in the world, the **Sydney Opera House** opens in 1973 in Sydney Harbour, Australia. Danish architect Jorn Utzon created the initial design, with work completed by an Australian team led by Peter Hall.

'73 interiors

IKEA
IKEA
TAJT text sidan 3
IKEA
KATALOG 1973
225:-
Impala hög/Nobel
455:-

In The News

Nixon Inaugurated

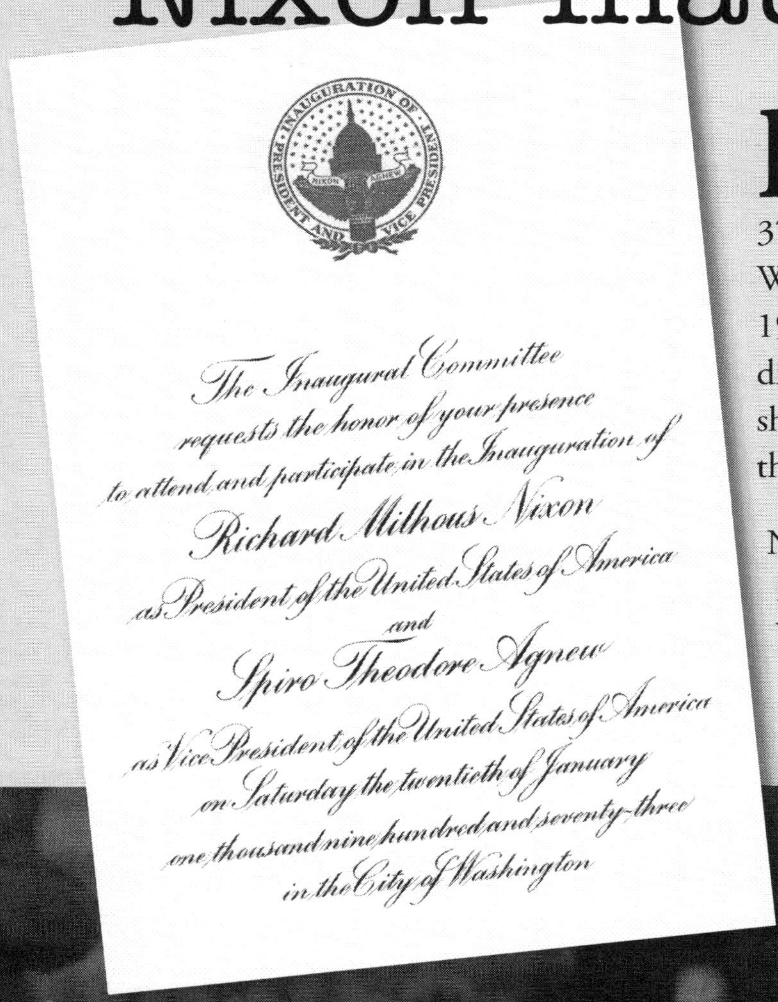

The Inaugural Committee
requests the honor of your presence
to attend and participate in the Inauguration of
Richard Milhous Nixon
as President of the United States of America
and
Spiro Theodore Agnew
as Vice President of the United States of America
on Saturday the twentieth of January
one thousand nine hundred and seventy-three
in the City of Washington

Richard M. Nixon is sworn into his second term in office as the 37th President of the United States in Washington, D.C. on January 20th, 1973. He will resign the presidency in disgrace the following year under the shadow of the Watergate scandal and the threat of impeachment.

Nixon remains the only person who has been twice sworn into both the Vice Presidency and the Presidency.

Nixon is sworn in by Chief Justice Warren Burger as Pat Nixon and Senate leader Marlow Cook look on.

POLITICS and WORLD EVENTS

Agnew Resigns

Under a cloud of corruption, Vice President **Spiro T. Agnew** resigns in October prior to pleading no contest to charges of income tax evasion in a Baltimore federal court. He is fined $10,000 and given 3 years' probation.

Following near-unanimous confirmation votes in the U.S. Senate and House of Representatives, House Minority leader **Gerald Ford** is sworn in as Vice President of the United States, replacing Agnew.

THE WATERGATE SCANDAL

Watergate burglars, known as the "White House Plumbers": James McCord, Jr., Virgilio Gonzalez, Frank Sturgis, Eugenio Martinez, Bernard Barker & chief operative G. Gordon Liddy.

Five men are arrested in June, 1972, for burglarizing the offices of the Democratic National Committee at the Washington D.C. Watergate Office Complex under the direction of the White House. President **Richard Nixon** and White House chief of staff **H. R. Haldeman** are later taped plotting to obstruct the FBI's investigation into the break-ins. In September of '72, a grand jury indicts the five office burglars, as well as operatives **Howard Hunt** and **G. Gordon Liddy**. In January, 1973, they are tried before Judge **John Sirica**, with some pleading guilty and some convicted by a jury. The Watergate Scandal leads to hearings, the conviction of 48 individuals and, eventually, the 1974 resignation of the President.

The WATERGATE **SCANDAL**

The Gaslighting of Martha Mitchell

Martha Mitchell

A controversial and often misrepresented figure during the Watergate Scandal, **Martha Mitchell** — wife of U.S. Attorney General and head of the Committee to Re-Elect the President (CRP), **John Mitchell** — is alarmed when she learns of the Nixon campaign's involvement in the Watergate burglary.

Despite her husband's strong-arm efforts to keep her in the dark and isolated, Martha makes telephone contact with United Press reporter **Helen Thomas** in June of 1972. That phone call is cut off abruptly, with John Mitchell later telling reporter Thomas that "[Martha] gets a little upset about politics..."

Days later a reportedly severely bruised Martha says that she had been tranquilized and held captive in a hotel to keep her quiet. Though she is dismissed by Nixon aides as an unstable woman with a drinking problem, she continues to speak candidly with the press about the campaign's dirty tricks. And, in 1973, she provides testimony in a civil suit against the CRP.

A photograph of the Watergate office complex entered into evidence at the burglary trial

The WATERGATE **SCANDAL**

Woodward, Bernstein and Deep Throat

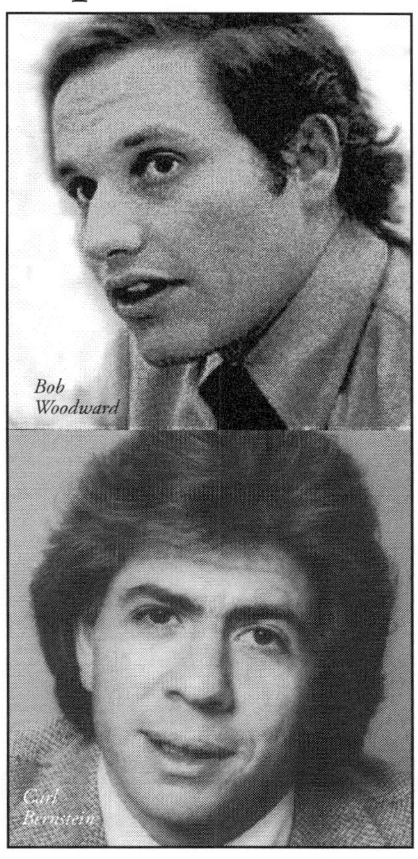

Bob Woodward

Carl Bernstein

Washington Post reporters **Bob Woodward** and **Carl Bernstein** are relatively unknown when they begin their investigative coverage of the Watergate break-in. They are aided in their work by a secret source nicknamed "Deep Throat," later revealed as FBI deputy director **Mark Felt**. In underground parking garage meetings, Deep Throat conveys the enormity of the coverup, including the involvement of former CIA officer **E. Howard Hunt**, the misappropriation of funds and the destruction of records. Woodward and Bernstein's buried scoops soon turn into increasingly consequential front-page headlines.

1973 ADVERTISEMENT

©VOLKSWAGEN OF AMERICA, INC.

Which man would you vote for?

Ah yes, what could be more dazzling than watching the candidates parade about, kissing babies and flashing winning smiles.

Consider the man in the top picture.

He promises to spend your tax dollars wisely.

But see how he spends his campaign dollars.

On a very fancy convertible.

Resplendent with genuine leather seats. A big 425-horsepower engine.

And a price tag that makes it one of the most expensive convertibles you can buy.

Now consider his opponent.

He promises to spend your tax dollars wisely.

But see how he spends his campaign dollars.

On a Volkswagen Convertible.

Resplendent with a hand-fitted top.

A warranty and four free diagnostic check-ups that cover you for 24 months or 24,000 miles.*

And a price tag that makes it one of the least expensive convertibles you can buy.

So maybe this year you'll find a politician who'll do what few politicians ever do:

Keep his promises before he's elected.

*If an owner maintains and services his vehicle in accordance with the Volkswagen maintenance schedule any factory part found to be defective in material or workmanship within 24 months or 24,000 miles, whichever comes first (except normal wear and tear and service items), will be repaired or replaced by any U.S. or Canadian Volkswagen Dealer. And this will be done free of charge. See your Volkswagen dealer for details.

The Watergate Scandal

The Hearings

Senate Watergate Committee chairman Sam Ervin.

In May, televised hearings into the Watergate scandal begin in the United States Senate. October 20th, the "Saturday Night Massacre," occurs when a panicked Richard Nixon orders Attorney General Elliot Richardson to fire Watergate Special Prosecutor Archibald Cox. Richardson refuses and resigns, leaving Solicitor General Robert Bork to fire Cox. Calls are raised for Nixon's impeachment. In November the existence of an 18 1/2-minute erased gap in one of the White House tape recordings comes to light.

Richard Nixon addressing reporters at a press conference in Orlando, Florida, on November 17th, 1973:

"...People have got to know whether or not their president is a crook. Well, I'm not a crook."

VIETNAMIZATION

With public opinion increasingly opposed to the Vietnam War, the **Richard Nixon** administration's Vietnamization policy, aimed at ending America's combat mission, achieved a limited rollback of Communist gains inside South Vietnam. The goal was primarily to provide the arms, training and funding for the South to fight and win its own war. Meanwhile, dead-locked peace talks in Paris between the U.S., North Vietnam, South Vietnam, and the Viet Cong entered their fifth year in 1972, finally beginning to make a bit of headway. In May of that year, Nixon makes a major concession by accepting a cease-fire in exchange for a U.S. military withdrawal without requiring North Vietnam to do the same. By 1972 year-end, the number of U.S. military personnel in South Vietnam totaled 24,200, down from more than 500,000 four years earlier.

January 15th, 1973 - U.S. President Richard Nixon announces the suspension of offensive action in North Vietnam.

January 27th - The Paris Peace Accords are signed, ending U.S. involvement in the Vietnam War.

March 17th - Many of the remaining United States soldiers begin to leave Vietnam.

August 15th - The U.S. bombing of Cambodia ends, officially halting 12 years of combat activity in Southeast Asia. American military operations in Laos, Cambodia, and North and South Vietnam cease.

DAILY NEWS 10¢

NEW YORK'S PICTURE NEWSPAPER ®

Vol. 54. No. 183 New York, N.Y. 10017, Wednesday, January 24, 1973 WEATHER: Sunny, windy and mild.

CEASEFIRE PACT!

Nixon: Fighting Ends Saturday; PWs to Be Freed in 60 Days

By JEFFREY ANTEVIL

Washington, Jan. 23 (News Bureau) —President Nixon announced tonight that the United States and North Vietnam have concluded an agreement to end the longest war in America's history and bring "peace with honor" to Vietnam.

IT'S ALL OVER

Thieu Sends Thanks to America

AN AUTHORIZED UNOFFICIAL PUBLICATION FOR THE U.S. ARMED FORCES OF THE PACIFIC COMMAND

Vol. 29, No. 28 Monday, Jan. 29, 1973

Peace Brings End to Draft 5 Mos. Early

CEASE-FIRE!

All GIs Out of Viet in 60 Days

The YOM KIPPUR WAR

On October 6, 1973, an Arab coalition led by Egypt and Syria launches a surprise attack against Israel on the Jewish holy day of Yom Kippur. The majority of the initial fighting occurs in the Israeli-occupied territories of the Sinai Peninsula and the Golan Heights, with Egypt attempting to gain control over the Suez Canal.

After three days, Israel halts Egypt's advance and pushes bach the Syrians. Within a week, Israel is shelling the outskirts of the Syrian capital, Damascus. By October 24th, Israeli armies have encircled the Egyptian army and moved close to Egypt's capital, Cairo. The world is alarmed when the United States provides material backing for Israel while the Soviet Union sides with the Arabs, stoking tensions between the superpowers. A United Nations-negotiated ceasefire largely ends the fighting by October 25th. Israel sustains up to 2,800 deaths, while Egyptian & Syrian deaths top 18,000. On November 11th, Israel and Egypt sign a U.S.-sponsored ceasefire accord.

Israeli Centurion tank in the Sinai.

Israeli soldiers.

Destroyed Israeli tank.

Egyptian troops cross the Suez Canal.

SST for '73 defies the stock description of "hot" performance machines, because we didn't have to strip it down to make all those horses perform like thoroughbreds. Quite the contrary. We made sure you'll get a smooth, complete-control ride by equipping the SST with the "Multiflex II" slide suspension at no extra cost. We combined it with our exclusive reinforced rubber "Positrack" for mountain-goat climbing agility. Then we added lots of little luxuries and extra performance features as standard equipment: Raised speedometer and tach. Tinted spoiler windshield. ThunderJet tapered seat. Padded engine cover. Front ski mounted shock absorbers. Powerful off-center headlamp. Engine cut-off switch.

Specifications

Displacement	Horsepower	Weight
295 c.c.	27 h.p.	328 lbs.
340 c.c.	32 h.p.	350 lbs.
440 c.c.	38 h.p.	355 lbs.

Bogie or "Multiflex II" slide suspension is standard equipment.

For purposes of product improvement, Sno Jet reserves the right to change or modify specifications without notice.

Hey big Blue!

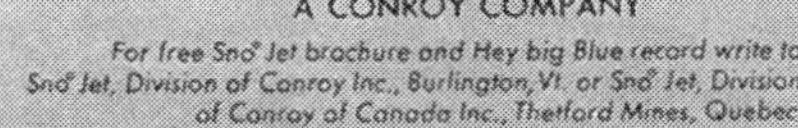

A CONROY COMPANY

For free Sno Jet brochure and Hey big Blue record write to Sno Jet, Division of Conroy Inc., Burlington, Vt. or Sno Jet, Division of Conroy of Canada Inc., Thetford Mines, Quebec.

ENERGY CRISIS

An oil embargo against countries supporting Israel in the Yom Kippur War is imposed by Saudi Arabia and OPEC (Organization of Petroleum-Exporting Countries) in October. The "oil shock" leads to gasoline shortages impacting the United States, Canada, Europe, Japan and other regions. By the end of the embargo early the following year, the price of crude oil will spike over 300%

A sign at an Oregon gas station warns of rationing.

SEPTEMBER 18 – The two German Republics, the **Federal Republic of Germany** (West Germany) and the **German Democratic Republic** (East Germany), are admitted to the United Nations.

The **Bahamas** are admitted to membership in the United Nations.

Operation Spring of Youth: In April, Israeli commandos land in speedboats on Lebanese beaches and conduct a surprise raid on Beirut, assassinating 3 leaders of the Palestinian Resistance Organization (PLO). Lebanese Prime Minister Saeb Salam resigns as a result.

Lillehammer Affair: In July, agents of the Israeli secret intelligence agency, Mossad, shoot and kill Moroccan waiter Ahmed Bouchiki as he walks with his wife in Lillehammer, Norway. The agents mistakenly believe Bouchiki to be a senior member of the Palestinian Black September Organization. When they learn of their error, nine of the hit squad members escape the country, while six are arrested. Though convicted and sentenced, they are released to Israel in 1975.

Ahmed Bouchiki

THE TROUBLES

Since the 1960s, Northern Ireland has been beset with strife arising from conflict between the Protestant Loyalists, who want Northern Ireland to remain within the United Kingdom, and the Catholic Irish Republicans, who want Northern Ireland to leave the United Kingdom and join a united Ireland. In 1972, explosions of political violence continue to rock the region. The troubles persist into 1973.

In April, a ship carrying 5 tons of weapons destined for the Provisional Irish Republican Army is intercepted by the Irish Naval Service. Six are arrested.

Elections for the Northern Ireland Assembly are held in June. For the first time, the Unionists and Nationalists will share power in Northern Ireland.

Three Provisional Irish Republican Army members escape from Mountjoy Prison, Dublin, aboard a hijacked helicopter which lands in the exercise yard. The escape results in all IRA prisoners being transferred to a maximum security prison.

Ulster Volunteer Force mural.

The 92nd U.S. Congress voted to send the proposed **Equal Rights Amendment** to the states for ratification on March 22, 1972. 22 state legislatures ratified the amendment and 8 more join in 1973. The ERA proposes to guarantee equal rights for all American citizens, regardless of sex.

THE WASHINGTON SUMMIT — **Richard Nixon**, U.S. Secretary of State **Henry Kissinger**, and Soviet leader **Leonid Brezhnev** convene in June to discuss ways to ease Cold War tensions. The talks build on the momentum of a number of arms agreements signed in Moscow in 1972, including the SALT I (Strategic Arms Limitation Talks) treaty and the Anti-Ballistic Missile Treaty.

A Value Added Tax (VAT) is introduced in the United Kingdom.

Erskine Hamilton Childers is elected the 4th President of Ireland.

The United Kingdom, the Republic of Ireland and Denmark enter the European Economic Community, which later becomes the European Union.

THE COD WAR: Britain announces that Royal Navy frigates will protect British trawlers fishing in the disputed 50 mile limit around Iceland.

Carl XVI Gustaf, becomes King of Sweden following the deaths of his grandfather, King Gustaf VI.

Greek dictator Georgios Papadopoulos is ousted in a military coup led by Brigadier General Dimitrios Ioannidis.

The Federal Republic of Germany and German Democratic Republic (GDR) recognize each other as sovereign states for the first time. Travel between the GDR and Poland, Czechoslovakia, and Hungary becomes visa-free.

NIXON SIGNS

U.S. President Richard Nixon signs...

- The Trans-Alaska Pipeline Authorization Act, authorizing construction of the Alaska Pipeline.
- The Endangered Species Act, to protect critically imperiled species from extinction.
- The Federal Highway Act, to provide road maintenance.

Congress overrides Nixon's veto of the War Powers Resolution, which limits presidential power to wage war without congressional approval.

1973 ADVERTISEMENT

OUR COUNTRY'S GASOLINE SHORTAGE

THE GREAT AMERICAN APPETITE.

America has a tremendous appetite. Not just for food, but for the natural resources that produce energy—gas and petroleum.

And we're running short of them, because the country is growing so fast, and using up its currently available resources even faster. People call it the Energy Crisis, and the current gasoline shortage is part of that crisis.

WHAT STANDARD IS DOING ABOUT THE SHORTAGE.

We want you to know that we're doing all we can to get as much gasoline to you as possible. In fact, we're making more gasoline than ever before in our history, up 15% in the last two years.

Standard refineries are running at over 95% of capacity (the practical maximum with available crude) This is well above the industry average.

What's more, our refinery through-put is up about 100,000 barrels a day since 1971. And we're now importing more foreign crude than in any other time in our history. Even though foreign crude is becoming more and more difficult to get.

Also, we want you to know we're working on new refining and conversion processes and new pipeline capabilities that will increase our output even more. And we're intensifying our search for crude oil to supply our refineries. This year, Standard and its affiliates will spend more on expansion, exploration and crude oil production than in any year before.

We wish we could say we'll solve the problem soon—and all by ourselves. But we can't do it alone. We need everyone's help. In the oil industry. In business. In government. And in every walk of American life.

WHAT YOU CAN DO.

If every American used just one gallon of gasoline less every week, there wouldn't be a shortage.

And there are many ways you can cut back. Walk a little more. Many times you can walk to the store when you have small purchases to make.

Form car pools. You and your neighbors probably go to a lot of the same places separately. Why not go together? To work. To the train. Even to meetings, parties and get-togethers.

Combine trips. Plan ahead so you don't have to make separate trips to the cleaners, and the drug store, and the grocery store.

Keep your car in top shape. A poorly tuned engine can reduce your gas mileage up to 10%.

Slow down. If you drive 50 miles an hour instead of 60, you can save about one gallon in ten. And take it easy when you start up. Jackrabbit starts eat up gasoline, too.

In summary, the gasoline shortage is no one individual's fault, but a combination of events. And it's up to all of us to find the solutions. And effect them.

Standard Oil Division of Amoco Oil Company

POLITICAL UPHEAVALS

Augusto Pinochet

September 11th

In Chile, the democratically elected government is overthrown in a violent military coup during a period of serious political instability. The Chilean Armed Forces shell the presidential palace, leading to the suicide by gunshot of President Salvador Allende. General Augusto Pinochet heads the military junta that governs Chile for the next 16 years, with tacit backing by the United States Central Intelligence Agency (CIA).

Salvador Allende

December 20th

Spanish Prime Minister Luis Carrero Blanco is assassinated in a bombing by the Basque separatist organization ETA.

March 10th

Sir Richard Sharples, Governor of Bermuda, is assassinated in a shooting inside Government House.

1973 ADVERTISEMENT

An AMF Roadmaster bicycle brings out the best in you. The lightest wheels in the world won't win the Tour de France, if you haven't the legs or the stamina.

But the Pacemaker 10-speed makes you look like a pro whether you want to make tracks or merely stay in condition. The tip-off is the name—Roadmaster. Built with the European touch for balance. And smooth, effortless motion.

And the kicky-looking toys like the Sling and the 3-wheeled Hot Seat stretch younger legs with fun that's made to last.

They're all AMF leisure time products. Made with a reverence for quality and value. The same goes for AMF's Slickcraft power boats, Voit balls or diving gear, Head skis, or Ben Hogan golf clubs.

So what if you don't qualify for the Six-Day Bike Races!

A Roadmaster bicycle could do wonders for your figure, and that's bringing out the best in you.

AMF Incorporated,
White Plains,
New York 10604.

AMF

AMF brings out the best in you.

A Year after placing the entire country under martial law in 1972, dictatorial

Philippines President Ferdinand Marcos

Philippines Sunday Express 10

FM DECLARES MARTIAL LAW

The nat'l situation in brief

But civilian gov't still functions; no military takeover

uses the declaration to extend his presidency beyond the term limits set by the Phillipine constitution, effectively becoming President for Life. And in July, Marcos' birthday gift to his wife, Imelda – the $22 million San Juanico Bridge linking the island of Samar to her home province – is dubbed a "white elephant" since the low traffic usage can never justify it's expense.

Ferdinand Marcos

Imelda Marcos

URUGUAY CRISIS

Against a backdrop of election fraud allegations and military insurrections, president **Juan María Bordaberry** dissolves the Parlaiment and commences a 12-year dictatorship in Uruguay.

The Ezeiza Massacre

June 20 – In Buenos Aires, Argentina, Peronist masses, gathered to rejoice over former president Juan Perón's return from an 18-year exile in Spain, are gunned down by right-wing snipers in camouflage. At least thirteen are killed while as many as 365 are wounded.

Peronist masses flood a platform where Juan Perón was to speak

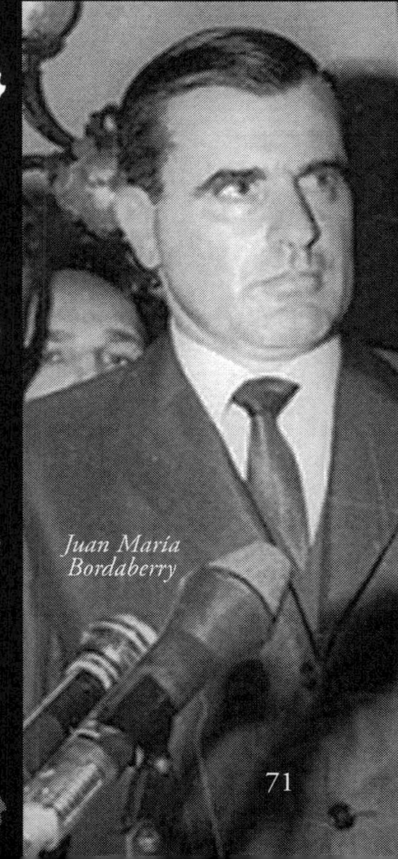
Juan María Bordaberry

1973 ADVERTISEMENT

We have only one proven source of energy for now...and the next 400 years

OIL

Known U.S. oil reserves may be depleted within 15 years. New discoveries are lagging. We are importing more and more foreign oil.

NUCLEAR

Promising but slow in developing. Atomic power *may be* our best bet in years to come. Now? No. Nuclear power today contributes less than one per cent of U.S. energy.

SOLAR

We would need perpetual sunlight. As yet, there's no practical way to store energy from the sun.

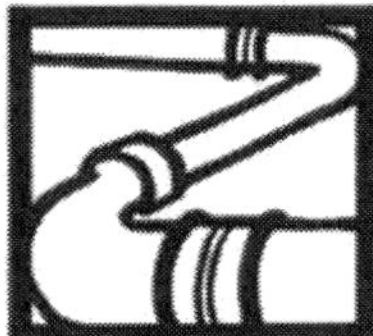

GAS

Our known gas reserves are dwindling fast. Within 15 years, demand may exceed existing domestic supply

WIND

Too primitive. Windmills still work in some areas, but they're unreliable and inefficient.

COAL

There's enough U.S. coal to last an estimated 400 years. Based on BTU values, coal makes up 88 per cent of the nation's energy reserves. Greater utilization of coal can keep our lights burning and our industry humming both now and for centuries ahead.

WATER

Only about 4 per cent of the nation's energy comes from water power. And we've already harnessed our best sources.

GEO-THERMAL

Heat from the interior of the earth has been tapped in a small way at demonstration sites. Interesting but impractical for now.

Coal is vital to steel

Coal is needed in vast quantities to make steel. And the steel industry is a large consumer of electric power, of which coal is by far the largest source. Bethlehem mined more than 13 million tons of coal last year, and most of this was used in our own blast furnaces.

Proposed legislation would restrict or ban surface mining

Surface-mined land can be reclaimed responsibly under present state reclamation laws. However, Federal legislation is now being considered that could unreasonably restrict or even ban surface mining of coal. About 20 per cent of Bethlehem's coal is surface-mined while more than 50 per cent of the nation's coal is surface-mined. If unreasonable restrictions on surface mining are enacted, the nation may be in trouble. That includes all coal users. And steel users. And all who use electric lights and appliances would feel the pinch.

Why restrict our most abundant fuel?

We favor legislation that will make it possible to meet the nation's energy needs and reasonable environmental goals at the same time. But why cut coal production by unreasonable restrictions on surface mining at a time when all other energy sources—except coal—are in critical supply?

THE THAI POPULAR *Uprising*

Thousands at Ratchadamnoen Avenue

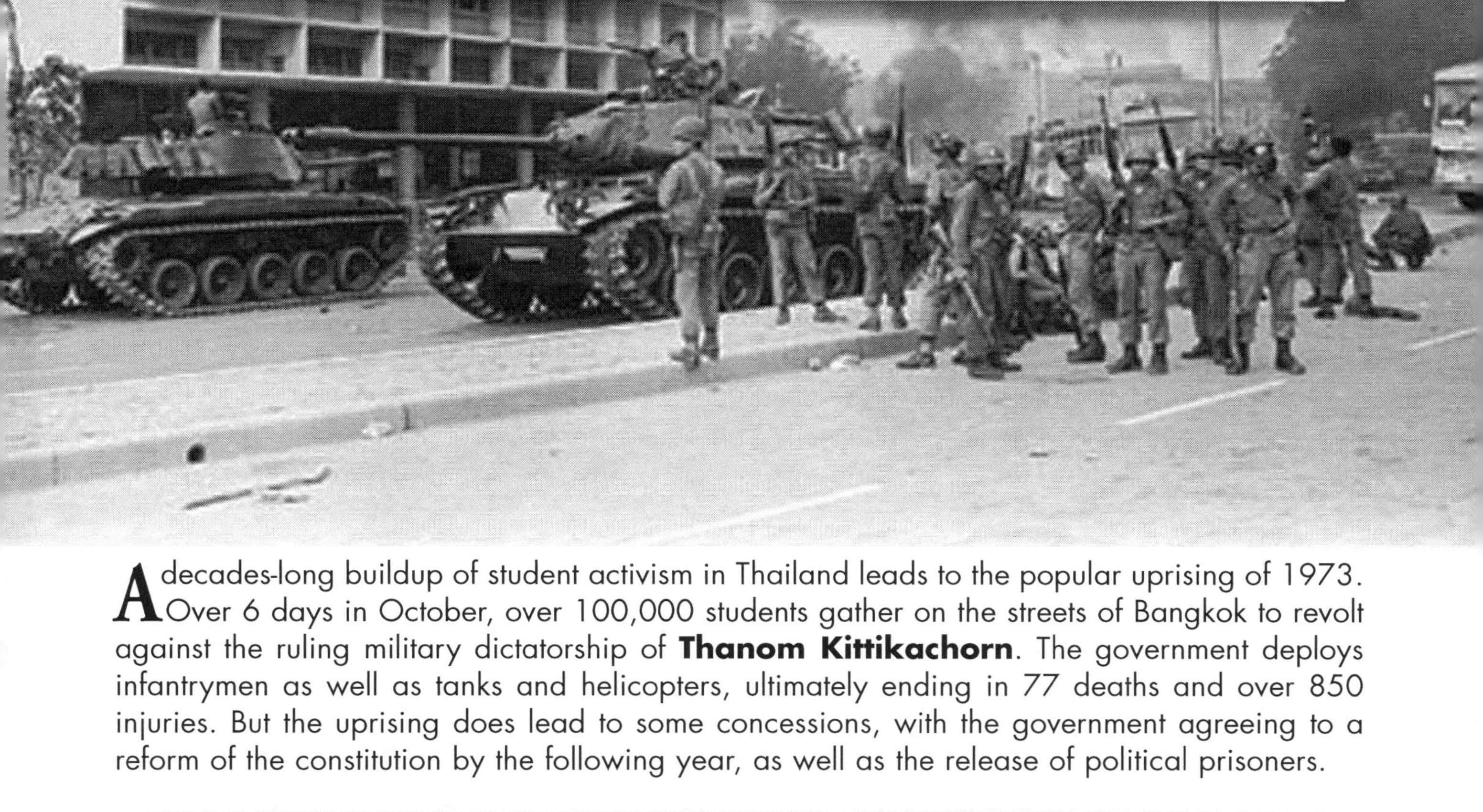

A decades-long buildup of student activism in Thailand leads to the popular uprising of 1973. Over 6 days in October, over 100,000 students gather on the streets of Bangkok to revolt against the ruling military dictatorship of **Thanom Kittikachorn**. The government deploys infantrymen as well as tanks and helicopters, ultimately ending in 77 deaths and over 850 injuries. But the uprising does lead to some concessions, with the government agreeing to a reform of the constitution by the following year, as well as the release of political prisoners.

Papua New Guinea, comprised of the eastern half of the island of New Guinea, gains self-government from Australia in December. With 839 languages, the country is the most linguistically diverse in the world.

1973 ADVERTISEMENT

Former civil servant Naim Talu is appointed to form the new government of Turkey following the resignation of Prime Minister Ferit Melen.

Also in Turkey, the Bosphorous Bridge in Istanbul is completed, linking Europe and Asia over the Bosphorous Strait. It becomes the 4th-longest suspension bridge in the world.

The Bosphorous Bridge on a Turkish banknote

TERRORISM

Carlos the Jackal

December 20th

Ilich Ramirez Sanchez, aka Venezuelan terrorist **Carlos the Jackal**, undertakes a failed assassination of Jewish businessman **Joseph Sieff** while Sieff is bathing in his British home. The attacker's first shot misses, then his gun jams and he flees.

In 1975, Carlos is sentenced to multiple life terms for committing at least 16 politically motivated murders.

The infamous Palestinian terrorist organization, **Black September**, attacks the Saudi Embassy in Khartoum in March, taking 10 hostages and killing 3. The following day, they attempt but fail to detonate 3 car bombs in New York during a visit by Israeli Prime Minister **Golda Meir**. And in August, they open fire on a passenger lounge at an airport in Athens, Greece, killing 3 and wounding 55.

Now...a little Motorola car stereo with a big voice

You may have seen a 2-channel, 8-track car stereo this small before, but listen to the range of that big, beautiful voice.

The Motorola Model TM213S is capable of reproducing audio frequencies of 50 to 10,000 hz, yet its size makes it ideal for under dash installation in many compact and foreign cars. (Speakers, optional extra.)

You get tone control, balance control, dual volume control, program selector with lighted program indicator, 12 transistors and 3 diodes, all in a compact solid state unit so small we can show it actual size in the ad.

Best of all, you get Motorola.

MOTOROLA®

SOMETHING ELSE in sound on wheels

People

Future U.S. Senator and presidential candidate, naval aviator lieutenant **John McCain** *is front and center among the P.O.W.s making their way home.*

Operation Homecoming

143 prisoners held by the Viet Cong are among the American troops making their way home in February with the end of U.S. involvement in the Vietnam war. Some looking gaunt and frail, many were subjected to physical and psychological torture including beatings, being hung upside down, made to stand for hours, and chained in total isolation.

In a wink to 1972's nude **Burt Reynolds** centerfold in ***Cosmopolitan*** magazine, comedienne **Phylis Diller** is dubbed "Miss Fun Fishing of 1973" when she poses for the centerfold of ***Field & Stream*** magazine.

Brando

While on his way to dinner in New York City with TV interviewer **Dick Cavett**, actor **Marlon Brando** takes a swing at the jaw of persisent papparazzi **Ron Gallela**. The photographer requires a hospital visit along with 9 stiches and a brace; Brando suffers an infection of his right hand.

In September, singer-songwriter **Stevie Wonder** recuperates in a Los Angeles hospital after 2 weeks in a North Carolina hospital, the result of an automobile accident which left him unconscious with a brain contusion.

Talk about unlikely besties! "Rifleman" actor **Chuck Connors** and Soviet party leader **Leonid Brezhnev** had such chemistry at a presidential party last year that Connors is heading to Moscow in '73 to hook up for some U.S.-Soviet sweet talk. It seems Brezhnev is a big fan of American western films.

On-again, off-again Hollywood couple **Liz Taylor** and **Richard Burton** are off-again, filing for a "friendly" divorce in Switzerland.

Yoko Ono and John Lennon

Former Beatle and New York City residents **John Lennon** & wife **Yoko Ono** battle a U.S. Immigration Department deportation order, sparked by their participation in anti-war demonstrations. The Lennons are aided in their efforts to remain in the country by New York City Mayor **John Lindsay** and numerous celebrities including **Bob Dylan**. Nevertheless, Lennon is denied permanent residency and ordered to leave in 60 days. The couple's fight continues until 1975, when the deportation order is overturned.

For her 1973 TV special, glamorous movie legend and songstress **Marlene Dietrich** is paid over $250,000. Nevertheless, she complains that CBS "works me to death... as if I were a machine."

1973 ADVERTISEMENT

You don't stay a champion by resting on your laurels.

Introducing the Triumph Spitfire 1500.

Win after win. Race after race. 30 times last year the Triumph Spitfire showed the world what a championship sports car is made of.

That was last year.

This year we have even bigger things in mind. And better.

This year's Spitfire has more engine than last year's racing champion. It's now a full 1½ litres.

To go along with the greater power, this year's new 1500 has a 2 in. wider rear track, a higher axle ratio (3.89 to 1) and a larger 7¼ in. clutch.

All of which means more traction, more stability, and more getaway power.

And to give you an even sportier sports car for your money, this year's Spitfire comes with a new racing style steering wheel, walnut dash and adjustable headrests, not to mention other less obvious, but significant improvements.

We know you don't stay a champion by resting on your laurels.

You'll know it too, the moment you test drive the new Spitfire 1500.

Triumph Spitfire 1500

We make sports cars for everybody.

Singer **Lena Horne** thrills her grandchildren and parents everywhere when she appears on the PBS-TV children's program, ***Sesame Street***. Horne joins **Kermit the Frog** in a rousing rendition of "It's Not Easy Being Green."

British dog trainer **Barbara Woodhouse** has dog-lovers everywhere exclaiming, ***"WALKIES!"*** Making the rounds of 20 U.S. TV shows in 21 days to promote her books, she instructs viewers that "You've got to be exciting to your dog, otherwise, he'll get depressed."

Legendary singer-dancer **Josephine Baker** leaves her villa on the French Riviera for a temporary return to New York City at the age of 67. There, she makes a splash at Carnegie Hall, reminding the audience of her scandalous Roaring Twenties performances when she sported only a short banana skirt. She remains more modestly clad for her '73 concert.

While sailing his 60-ft. yacht at Newport Beach, Calif., Arizona Senator and former presidential candidate **Barry Goldwater** hears a woman screaming after she is thrown into the water from her speedboat. Goldwater dives into the water, rescues a North Hollywood couple, and delivers them safely to the harbor police.

Nepal's **Shambu Tamang** becomes the youngest person to climb to the summit of Mount Everest at the age of 16.

California's **Yvonne Brathwaite Burke** becomes the first member of the U.S. House of Representatives to be granted maternity leave.

Former Harvard lecturer and LSD advocate **Timothy Leary**, famous for advocating all to "Turn on, tune in, drop out", has been on the lam from various drug charges for years. He is finally apprehended by U.S. narcs who hustle him to Los Angeles and a 5-year prison sentence.

1973 ADVERTISEMENT

LED ZEPPELIN 5017 Atlantic
Houses Of The Holy

ISAAC HAYES 0653 Enterprise
Live At The Sahara Tahoe 2 LPs & 2 tapes

ELTON JOHN 8441 MCA
Don't Shoot Me I'm Only The Piano Player

J. GEILS BAND 5215 Atlantic
Bloodshot

URIAH HEEP 0208 Mercury
Live 2 LPs & 2 tapes

AL GREEN 5637 Hi
Call Me

ANNE MURRAY 4739 Capitol
Danny's Song

JOAN BAEZ 3186 Vanguard
Greatest Hits

SPINNERS 5223 Atlantic

SHA NA NA 0729 Kama Sutra 2 LPs & 2 tapes
Golden Age Of Rock And Roll

STAPLE SINGERS 6452 Stax
Be What You Are

STEVIE WONDER 6692 Tamla
Talking Book

GODSPELL 7914 Bell
Movie Soundtrack

NEIL DIAMOND 0962 MCA
Hot August Night 2 LPs & 2 tapes

BLOODSTONE 5678 London
Natural High

HELEN REDDY 4689 Capitol
I Am Woman

NO LIMIT *LPs or Tapes Cartridge or Cassette* 99¢ EACH!

TAKE AS MANY AS YOU WANT— MINIMUM OF 5 SELECTIONS

AT LAST A RECORD & TAPE CLUB WITH NO "OBLIGATIONS"—ONLY BENEFITS

Yes, now you can TAKE ALL YOU WANT of these Great Top Hits—LPs, 8-Track Tape Cartridges or Cassettes—FOR ONLY 99¢ EACH! And get FREE Lifetime Membership too (millions paid $5.00 and more to join). All this with absolutely NO OBLIGATION to buy anything ever! And this is JUST AN INTRODUCTION to the kind of GIANT SAVINGS you can enjoy everyday FROM THE INSTANT YOU JOIN. Because we are not OWNED . . . NOT CONTROLLED . . . NOT SUBSIDIZED by any record or tape manufacturer anywhere, you always get the world's lowest prices—GUARANTEED DISCOUNTS UP TO 81%—on records and tapes of ALL LABELS!

See Why 4,000,000 Record and Tape Buyers Paid a Lifetime Membership Fee to Join Record Club of America when Other Clubs Would Have Accepted Them FREE!

Compare and see!	RECORD CLUB OF AMERICA	Columbia Record/Tape Clubs (as advertised in Oui Jan. '73)	RCA Record/Tape Clubs (as advertised in TV Guide Aug. '72)	Capitol Record/Tape Clubs (as advertised in Seventeen Nov. '72)	Citadel Record Club (as advertised in Parade July '72)
CAN YOU CHOOSE FROM ALL LABELS?	**YES!** Choose recordings on any label. No exceptions! Over 300 different manufacturers including Capitol, Columbia, RCA, Angel, London, etc.	NO	NO	NO	NO
CAN YOU PICK LPs AND TAPES, INCLUDING CARTRIDGE AND CASSETTE TAPES?	**YES!** Pick LPs OR 8-track tape cartridges OR tape cassettes. No restrictions. No additional membership fee or separate "division" to join!	NO	NO	NO	NO
MUST YOU BUY A "MINIMUM" NUMBER OF LPs OR TAPES? HOW MANY?	**NONE!** No obligations! No yearly quota! Take as many, as few, or nothing at all if you so decide.	11 LPs/ 8 Tapes	12 LPs/ 12 Tapes	12 LPs/ 10 Tapes	12 LPs
HOW MUCH MUST YOU SPEND TO FULFILL YOUR LEGAL OBLIGATION?	**ZERO DOLLARS!** You don't have to spend a penny—because you're not "legally obligated" to buy even a single record or tape!	$54.61 to $85.10	$69.95 to $105.95	$70.03 to $94.03	$56.25 to $74.25
CAN YOU BUY ANY LP OR TAPE YOU WANT AT A DISCOUNT?	**ALWAYS!** Guaranteed discounts up to 81% on LPs and tapes of ALL LABELS!	NO	NO	NO	NO
DO YOU EVER RECEIVE UNORDERED LPs OR TAPES?	**NEVER!** There are no cards which you must return. Only the records and tapes you want are sent — and only when you ask us to send them.	YES	YES	YES	YES

Record Club of America— The World's Largest and Lowest Priced Record And Tape Club

NEW ENGLAND CONSERVATORY RAGTIME ENSEMBLE/SCHULLER 4747 Angel
Scott Joplin—The Red Back Book

SERGIO MENDES & BRASIL '77 7930 Bell
Love Music

DIANA ROSS 0679 Motown 2 LPs & 2 tapes
Lady Sings The Blues

JERRY LEE LEWIS 0216 Mercury 2 LPs & 2 tapes
The Session

GLADYS KNIGHT & THE PIPS 6627 Soul
Neither One Of Us

FIFTH DIMENSION 7880 Bell
Living Together, Growing Together

KRIS KRISTOFFERSON 5801 Monument
Jesus Was A Capricorn

TEMPTATIONS 6619 Gordy
Masterpiece

HISTORY OF THE GRATEFUL DEAD 9407 Pride

VICKI LAWRENCE 7955 Bell
The Night The Lights Went Out In Georgia

BEST OF B.B. KING 1503 ABC

DONNY OSMOND 9241 MGM
Alone Together

MAHLER* 0794 London 2 LPs
8th Symphony—Solti

JOHN DAVIDSON 2162 Mercury
Well, Here I Am

MANDRILL 5306 Polydor
Composite Truth

CLAUDINE LONGET 9399 Barnaby
Let's Spend The Night Together

INTRODUCING LOBO 7948 Big Tree

WATTSTAX 2 LPs & 2 tapes 0620 Stax

MOODY BLUES 5611 Threshold
Seventh Sojourn

EDWARD BEAR 4697 Capitol

DAWN 7896 Bell
Tuneweaving

MORE GREAT HITS TO CHOOSE FROM

JOHN MAYALL Down The Line
2 LPs & 2 tapes 0836
LARRY CORYELL Offering 3012
VERDI* Rigoletto—London
Symphony 3 LPs 0844
KENNY ROGERS & THE FIRST
EDITION Backroads 9290
THE BAND Rock Of Ages
2 LPs & 2 tapes 0109
THE OSMONDS Crazy Horses 9126
FIFTH DIMENSION
Greatest Hits On Earth 7823
HEAVY CREAM 2 LPs & 2 tapes 0919
PIPPIN Original Cast 6726
MAMAS & PAPAS 20 Golden Hits
2 LPs & 2 tapes 0612
DONIZETTI* Lucia Di Lammermoor—
Sutherland 3 LPs 0877
JOAN BAEZ Ballad Book
2 LPs & 2 tapes 0380
PARTRIDGE FAMILY At Home
With Their Greatest Hits 7724
DIONNE WARWICKE STORY
A Decade Of Gold
2 LPs & 2 tapes 0273
CAT STEVENS Matthew & Son/
New Masters 2 LPs & 2 tapes 0885
KRIS KRISTOFFERSON
Me And Bobby McGee 5835
GLEN TRAVIS CAMPBELL 4655
2001: A SPACE ODYSSEY
Soundtrack 9050
SOVIET ARMY CHORUS & BAND*
On Parade 8656
ANNE MURRAY Annie 4663
B. J. THOMAS Greatest Hits
Volume 1 2634
GEORGE SZELL
MEMORIAL ALBUM* 7310
HISTORY OF THE
RIGHTEOUS BROTHERS 9340
BEST OF AN ERA
12 Great Rock Hits 7328
SHOSTAKOVICH* Symphony #5—
Kondrashin 8664
BLOODROCK Passage 4614
STEVE & EYDIE Feelin' 9258
JIM CROCE Life And Times 1149
TONY BENNETT Listen Easy 9274
ARTHUR FIEDLER &
THE BOSTON POPS
Bacharach-David Songbook 5371
B.J. THOMAS Country 2618
STEREO TEST RECORD* 7070
CASHMAN & WEST
A Song Or Two 1321
GREAT WALTZ
Original Soundtrack 9308
THE SOUNDS OF LOVE A To Zzzz . . . 7278
METROPOLITAN OPERA GALA*
Honoring Sir Rudolph Bing 5405
NEW SEEKERS
Come Softly To Me 9316
BEST OF JOHN COLTRANE
2 LPs & 2 tapes 0745

* These Selections Not Available In Tape

MARVIN GAYE Trouble Man Soundtrack 6700 Tamla
SIEGEL-SCHWALL BAND & SAN FRANSISCO SYMPHONY ORCH. Pieces For Blues Band & Orch 5330 DGG
LOST HORIZON Soundtrack 7906 Bell
BEST OF THE JAMES GANG 1024 ABC

ROY BUCHANAN Second Album 5348 Polydor
FOUR TOPS Keeper Of The Castle 1123 ABC/Dunhill
TEMPTATIONS All Directions 6684 Gordy
HURRICANE SMITH 4705 Capitol

GILBERT O'SULLIVAN Back To Front 5645 MAM
MOODY BLUES Days Of Future Passed 5520 Deram
JACKSON FIVE Skywriter 6718 Motown
LOBO Of A Simple Man 7922 Big Tree

NO OBLIGATION

To Buy Anything Ever!

Special FREE Lifetime Membership!

ISAAC HAYES Shaft 2 LPs & 2 tapes 0638
A TRIBUTE TO BURT BACHARACH 2790
CRUISIN' 1962 Rock 'N' Roll History 6809
CRUISIN' 1960 Rock 'N' Roll History 3889
WURST OF P.D.Q. BACH 2 LPs & 2 tapes 0364
HISTORY OF THE GUESS WHO 9324
STAPLE SINGERS Bealtitude: Respect Yourself 6437
BEST OF TIM HARDIN 9332
BOOTS RANDOLPH Plays The Great Hits Of Today 5827
JAMES TAYLOR & THE FLYING MACHINE 3707
BEST OF THE BEST OF MERLE HAGGARD 4648
RAMSEY LEWIS The Groover 6908
JOAN BAEZ 5 3087
BEETHOVEN Piano Sonatas 7047
PETULA CLARK Now 9357
THE GRASS ROOTS Their 16 Greatest Hits 1198
RAVEL Bolero DEBUSSY Afternoon Of A Faun 7286
BEST OF BILLIE HOLIDAY 9209
BEETHOVEN Symphony #9 7252
THE JOEY HEATHERTON ALBUM 9233
KRIS KRISTOFFERSON The Silver-Tongued Devil And I 5843
WES MONTGOMERY Just Walkin' 9183
B.J. THOMAS Greatest Hits Volume 2 2774
MUSIC OF CHINA TODAY* 2 LPs 0067
GUESS WHO Born In Canada 2642
ALBERT KING I'll Play The Blues For You 6445
DOCTOR ZHIVAGO Original Soundtrack 9365
MICHEL LEGRAND Brian's Song 7864
TCHAIKOVSKY 1812 Overture 7005
PAUL MAURIAT Theme From A Summer Place 9175
CHUCK BERRY'S GOLDEN DECADE Volume 2 2LPs & 2 tapes 0703
BERLIOZ* Harold In Italy —Oistrakh 8672
RIGHTEOUS BROTHERS 14 Greatest Hits 9373
JOAN BAEZ & BOB DYLAN Newport Folk Festival 3152
ROBERT GOULET I Never Did As I Was Told 9068
ENVIRONMENTAL SOUNDS 7260
THE WORLD OF BOOTS RANDOLPH 5850
ROY BUCHANAN 5397
MOTHERS OF INVENTION Freak Out 2 LPs & 2 tapes 0869
CHOPIN Polonaises 7054
WIZARD OF OZ Original Soundtrack 9167
RICHARD HARRIS The Love Album 1164

* These Selections Not Available In Tape

DON McLEAN 4010 United Artists
OHIO PLAYERS Pleasure 6817 Westbound
ERIC CLAPTON 5355 Polydor
CHUCK BERRY'S GOLDEN DECADE 2 LPs & 2 tapes 0695 Chess
THREE DOG NIGHT Seven Separate Fools 1404 ABC/Dunhill
STRAUSS* Also Sprach Zarathustra —Mehta 5660 London
URIAH HEEP The Magician's Birthday 2014 Mercury
THE POWER OF JOE SIMON 5363 Spring
VICTORIA DE LOS ANGELES* Songs Of The Auvergne 4721 Angel
SMOKEY ROBINSON & THE MIRACLES 1957-1972 2 LPs & 2 tapes 0717 Tamla
DAVID BOWIE Images 2 LPs & 2 tapes 0786 London
CHUCK BERRY The London Sessions 6882 Chess
GRAND FUNK RAILROAD Phoenix 4606 Capitol
STEPPENWOLF 16 Greatest Hits 1214 ABC/Dunhill
THE SYLVERS 9268 Pride
ROD STEWART Never A Dull Moment 2154 Mercury
STEVE MILLER BAND Anthology 2 LPs & 2 tapes 0117 Capitol
RICHARD HARRIS His Greatest Performances 1222 ABC/Dunhill
NEW SEEKERS Pinball Wizards 9282 MGM/Verve
ERIC CLAPTON At His Best 2 LPs & 2 tapes 0901 Polydor
RASPBERRIES FRESH 4713 Capitol

GREATEST NEW MEMBER OFFER IN RECORD AND TAPE HISTORY

Other record and tape clubs make you choose from just a few labels. They make you buy up to 12 records and tapes a year. And if you don't return their monthly IBM cards, they send you an item you don't want and a bill for up to $8.38. At Record Club of America we've BANISHED AUTOMATIC SHIPMENTS FOREVER! You NEVER receive an unordered recording. NEVER have to return any cards. You get only WHAT YOU WANT...WHEN YOU WANT IT. And always at the WORLD'S LOWEST PRICES!

GET LPs ON ALL LABELS FOR $1.69 OR LESS...TAPES $1.99

We're the world's largest ALL LABEL Record and Tape Club, so we can give you the WORLD'S LOWEST PRICES on all records and tapes made. Guaranteed discounts up to 81%! IMAGINE PAYING $1.69 AVERAGE PRICE FOR TOP HIT $5.98 STEREO LPs...including the very latest New Releases. $1.99 FOR $6.98 STEREO TAPE CARTRIDGES AND CASSETTES. Yet that's exactly the Sale Offer mailing now to members even as you read this! You can CASH IN ON THESE GIANT SAVINGS too—the instant you join—not after fulfilling some annoying "obligation" like other clubs.

SAVE ON THIS SPECIAL INTRODUCTORY OFFER

Join Record Club of America today and TAKE AS MANY LPs or TAPES shown here AS YOU WANT (minimum of 5—no duplicate selections) FOR ONLY 99¢ EACH! Mail coupon with check or money order for 99¢ for each of your recordings (a bill for the Club's standard mailing and handling fee will be sent later). Receive by return mail your recordings plus incredible "BUY 1, GET 2 FREE" offer on 100's of Top Hit LPs and Tapes. New super-discount FREE or Dividend offer every 21 days. Remember, you receive FREE Lifetime Membership (never pay another Club fee for the rest of your life) with absolutely NO OBLIGATION to buy anything ever!

ACT NOW AND YOU GET FREE

FREE—All-Label Lifetime Discount Membership Card. FREE—Giant Master Discount Catalog of all readily available records and tapes. FREE—subscriptions to Disc & Tape Guide Magazine and the WAREHOUSE Catalog of hip products. YOUR ORDER COMPUTER PROCESSED FOR EXPRESS SERVICE DELIVERY—no shipping on cycle! 100% money-back guarantee if items are returned within 10 days. AND NOW YOU CAN CHARGE IT TOO!

RECORD CLUB OF AMERICA

CLUB HEADQUARTERS / YORK, PENNSYLVANIA 17405 VO93D

YES—Rush me my Lifetime Membership Discount Card, Giant All-Label Master Discount Catalog, plus subscriptions to Disc & Tape Guide Magazine and the WAREHOUSE ™ Catalog. Also send me the ____ LPs or ____ Tapes indicated below (minimum of 5 selections, no duplicate selections) with a bill for the Club's standard mailing and handling fee. I enclose 99¢ for EACH of my recordings for a total of $______. I am not obligated to buy any records or tapes ever—no yearly quota. If not completely delighted I may return above items within 10 days for an immediate refund. IMPORTANT: 2 or 3 LP or Tape sets count as 2 or 3 selections; selections marked ★ are not available on tape.

ENTER LP OR TAPE NUMBERS BELOW—Sorry, No Mixing AP 2

____ I am attaching a separate sheet of paper to list additional selections

IMPORTANT! YOU MUST CHECK ONE: ☐ LP or ☐ 8 TRACK or ☐ CASSETTE

Mr. Mrs. Miss

RT RR RD SR Box or P.O. Box

Street Apt

City State Zip

APO & FPO ADDRESSES, PLEASE FILL IN YOUR SOCIAL SECURITY NO.

CHARGE IT to my credit card. I am charging the above total (mailing and handling fee will be added). Check one: ☐ Master Charge ☐ American Express ☐ BankAmericard ☐ Diners Club

Acct. # Expiration Date

CANADIANS mail coupon to above address. Prices and listings may vary slightly. Orders will be serviced in Canada by Record Club of Canada

ENQUIRING MINDS want to KNOW

NATIONAL ENQUIRER 25¢
How to Use Anxiety To Your Advantage
LARGEST CIRCULATION OF ANY PAPER IN AMERICA
MYSTERIOUS WAVE OF UFOs REPORTED IN MASS SIGHTING
What You Should Know About the Dangers in Your Medicine Cabinet page 21
Top Psychic's New Predictions for Enquirer Readers page 5
6 Actresses Tell Why Sex Appeal Doesn't Have to End at 40 page 38

Astounding Breakthrough Revealed:
Scientists Are Communicating With The Dead
Messages From Beyond The Grave
Old Kids About The Effects Drugs ergarten
Giving Away $1 Billion usands Of Americans

NATIONAL ENQUIRER 20¢
How to Save on Gas & Electric Bills
'Cheat-Proof' Experiments at Stanford Research Institute Baffle Scientists Who Confirm 26-Year-Old's...
SUPERNATURAL POWER
Exclusive!

Midnight
FEBRUARY 5, 1973
ckie Horrified Because...
ohn Kennedy Jr arries A Knife or Protection gainst Kidnap Attempts

NATIONAL ENQUIRER 20¢
Conversation: How It Reveals Personality
Professor of Pharmacology at the Univ. of California Charges:
WRONGLY PRESCRIBED DRUGS
· KILL 24,000 A YEAR
· HOSPITALIZE 3,600,000
The Discovery That Brings New Hope for the Overweight page 22

NATIONAL ENQUIRER 20¢
How to Become A Self-Starter
Dramatic Warning By Panel of Experts—TV Is a...
MARRIAGE KILLER
Another ENQUIRER Exclusive
What the Stars Foretell For Lucky page 10
Taylor's Fight ave Her Marriage centerfold
to Relieve sions page 18
'I QUIT'
Archie Bunker's 'All in the Family' Shock

ENQUIRER 20¢
How You Can Learn to Loaf
FIRST TIME IN MEDICAL HISTORY
MAN BECOMES PREGNANT AFTER RECEIVING OVARY TRANSPLANT
Common Drugs Can Cause Birth Defects page 3
Senator Proxmire's Simple Method for Staying Healthy And Saving Money page 20
Phyllis Diller on Marriage: 'It's All Over. I've Had It!'

NATIONAL ENQUIRER 20¢
Your Body Clock Can Help You Enjoy Life
10 Leading Psychics Reveal Their...
PREDICTIONS FOR 1973

Tom Bradley defeats incumbent Sam Yorty to become the first black mayor of Los Angeles and the second black mayor of a major U.S. city. He will serve for 20 years, the longest tenure of any L.A. mayor. Bradley campaigns on the development of a long-range growth plan, including a rapid-transit system.

ROYAL CHRONICLES

On November 26th, 22-year-old **Princess Anne**, the second of Queen Elizabeth's four children, marries **Mark Anthony Peter Phillips**, 25, commoner captain in the Queen's Dragoon Guards.

Queen Elizabeth II and the **Duke of Edinburgh** embark on a Royal Tour of Canada, visiting Toronto, Ontario, and many other locales on their first official state visit to the constitutional monarchy.

Carl XVI Gustaf becomes the King of Sweden with the death of his grandfather, **Gustaf VI Adolf** on Sseptember 15th.

OT CROSS CRIME SCENE DO

John Paul Getty III

July 10, 1973 - 16-year-old **John Paul Getty III**, the grandson of the oil tycoon, is kidnapped in Rome and held for $17 million ransom. **J. Paul Getty** refuses to pay, but after a severed ear is sent to a newspaper, $2.2 million is negotiated and, in December, young Getty is freed. 9 kidnappers, some of whom are members of an organized crime ring, are eventually apprehended.

August, 1973 - A bank robber takes 4 people hostage in Norrmalmstorg, Stockholm, Sweden. During their week-long ordeal, the hostages begin to sympathize with the robber, **Jan-Erik Olsson**, leading to the phenomenon that comes to be known as "Stockholm Syndrome," in which hostages develop a psychological bond with their captors.

David Akeman is better known as **Stringbean**, a beloved banjo-plucking member of the TV show "Hee-Haw," and a favorite musician featured at the Grand Ole Opry. Despite his success, Akeman and his wife stick to a modest lifestyle in a small cabin near Ridgetop, Tennessee, where they enjoy hunting and fishing.

On November 10th — a Saturday night — the couple return home after a night at the Grand Ole Opry, when they are shot dead by killers who are ransacking their home, looking for money. 23-year-old cousins **John Brown** and **Marvin Brown** are arrested for the murders.

Stringbean

June 24, 1973 - The **UpStairs Lounge Arson Attack** is an as-yet unsolved attack on a 2nd-floor gay bar in New Orleans, LA, in which 32 patrons die of smoke inhalation. The chief suspect, never charged, commits suicide in 1974.

Dayton, OH - Seven die and 14 are injured in a series of racist attacks against African-American men between 1972 and 1975. The shooter, **Neal Bradley Long**, known as the **Shotgun Slayer**, is arrested, convicted and dies in prison in 1998.

Los Angeles,CA - At least 7 women are killed between 1972 and 1986 by the **Southland Strangler**, also known as the **Westside Rapist**. It is not until 2009 that police arrest an insurance claims adjuster named **John Floyd Thomas**, thanks to a DNA sample. Thomas is convicted and sentenced to life in prison for 7 murders, though he may have killed as many as 21 women.

Thomas

NOT CROSS CRIME SCENE

SERIAL KILLERS

The Alphabet Murders (also known as the Double Initial Murders) are an unsolved series of child murders which occured between 1971 and 1973 in Rochester, New York. All three victims of the Alphabet Murders are girls aged ten or eleven, whose surname begins with the same letter as that of her first name. Each victim has been sexually assaulted and murdered by strangulation before her body is discarded in or near a town also beginning with same letter as her initials.

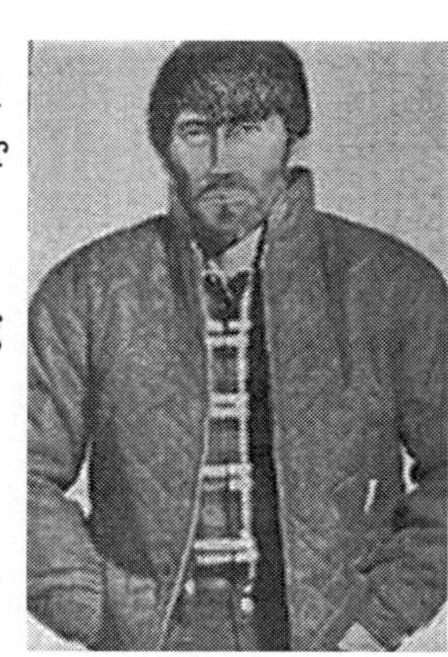

Artist's rendering of an unknown individual seen with victim Michelle Maenza prior to her murder.

Rodney James Alcala commenced a rape and muder spree spanning the country and including at least 8 victims between 1971 and 1979, though the true victim count remains unknown, and could be much higher. Alcala compiled a collection of more than 1,000 photographs of women and teenage girls, many in sexually explicit poses. He tortured his victims before raping and strangling them. He is known as the **Dating Game Killer** because of his 1978 appearance on that television game show in the midst of his murder spree. (The bachelorette refused their date, calling him "creepy.")

Alcala is arrested in late 1979 and ultimately sentenced to death in California and 25 years to life in New York. He will die in prison in 2021 at the age of 77.

Alcala

Kraft sentenced to death in 1989

Variously known as the **Scorecard Killer**, for coded lists he kept, the **Southern California Strangler,** and the **Freeway Killer**, **Randy Kraft** is believed to have raped, tortured and killed a total of 67 victims. between 1971 and 1983. His victims were males between the ages of 13 through their twenties. Many of his victims had been US Marines and most had high levels of alcohol and tranquilizers in their blood systems.

He is ultimately charged with and convicted of sixteen homicides. As of 2022, he remains incarcerated on death row at San Quentin State Prison, California.

1973 ADVERTISEMENT

The first true self-adjusting color set ever.

The amazing Sylvania GT-Matic.

The key

So automatic we lock up the controls.

If you've seen Perry Como describe this new Sylvania color set on TV, you know what we have here.

You may never have to correct the GT-Matic™ picture or color.

This is not the one-button tuning of other sets. GT-Matic is no-button color tuning. If you want to change anything on your own, fine. The set is built to remember the way you like it from then on.

Adjusts itself with revolutionary memory circuits.

Special memory circuits are designed to constantly correct your pictures for brightness, contrast, tint, color level, even vertical and horizontal hold. GT-Matic watches the picture while you watch the program.

This set even remembers the color you like to see in faces, and when that isn't the color that's coming in, GT-Matic goes to work.

(Everything you want in color TV —100% solid state, ChroMatrix II™ picture tube—*and GT-Matic, too.*)

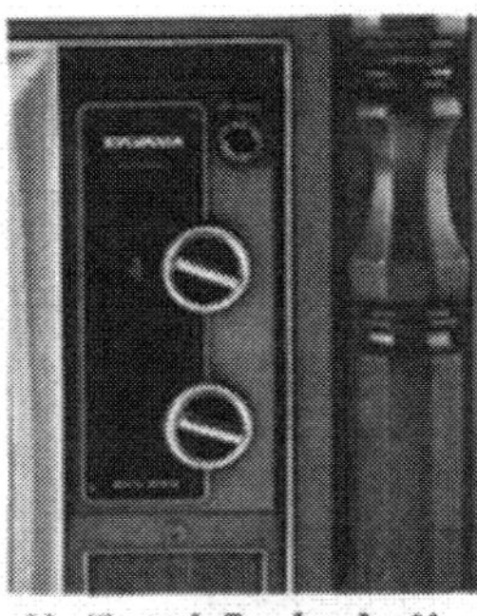

No "handy" color button
Or vertical button
Or tint button
Or horizontal button
Or AFC button
Or brightness button
Or contrast button
Or permatint button

Please do not try to help.

Just turn it on and change channels. The GT-Matic set is not only preset by us—it resets itself to help take care of all sorts of problems: airplanes, man-made electrical noise, even many transmitter problems. Sizes are 19," 21" and 25" (diagonal) and you have 24 models to choose from.

Take it from Perry Como: "GTE Sylvania's invented nothing to do."

GTE SYLVANIA

Simulated TV Picture

So automatic the controls are locked inside.
(Perry Como in a scene from his latest commercial.)

famous births

David Muir

Monica Lewinsky

Google founder Larry Page

Rachel Maddow

Heidi Klum

Mario Lopez

Tyra Banks

David Blaine

MOST ADMIRED **MAN**: **Henry Kissinger** U.S. Secretary of State

MOST ADMIRED **WOMAN**: **Golda Meir** Israeli Prime Minister

Kissinger Meir

Passings

LBJ

LYNDON B. JOHNSON, 64 - The 36th President of the United States (1963-1969). Sworn in following the assassination of John F. Kennedy, LBJ focused on expanding civil rights, access to healthcare, and aid to education. His accomplishments in domestic policy are often overshadowed by the Vietnam War mire.

DAVID BEN-GURION, 87 - Israel's first Prime Minister.

EDDIE RICKENBACKER, 82 - American World War I flying ace.

FRANK COSTELLO,82 - Luciano family crime boss.

ALBERT DeSALVO, 42 - The infamous serial killer, Boston Strangler.

TIME MAN OF THE YEAR

John Sirica
Watergate Judge

1973 ADVERTISEMENT

The Men's Lib Watch

Is your wristwatch a time chauvinist? Does it demand too much of your time for the time it gives? With the boredom of winding it every day? And the drudgery of turning the hands through 24 hours, just to reset the date? (Maybe it doesn't even tell you the date. Or the day.) ¶ Well, Bulova has a watch that will give you freedom, now. A self-winding date and day watch. With an instant change feature that lets you adjust end-of-month dates with a pull and push of the stem. ¶ It's water and shock resistant (to help free you from worrying about its health). And it has a time-tested Bulova movement (to help free you from worrying about its reliability). ¶ The Instant Change Date and Day Automatic. In styles ranging from radical to conservative. At all fine jewelry and department stores.

BULOVA. These days the right time isn't enough.

From left to right: #12620—#11002—#11633—#12006. These styles and others from $65. © Bulova Watch Co., Inc.

Human Interest

THE BATTLE OF THE SEXES

September 20th, 1973

The largest live audience ever to see a tennis match tune in to watch 55-year-old **Bobby Riggs** take on 29-year-old **Billie Jean King** at the Houston Astrodome. Riggs, ranked #1 in the 1940s, had been taunting and challenging female players. Striking a blow for women in sports, King, the #1 female player, wins the match in straight sets, 6–4, 6–4, 6–3. The global TV audience is estimated at 90 million.

Skyjacking

A PARTIAL LISTING of 1973 EVENTS

April 24 • A man with a bomb tries to hijack Aeroflot flight Tu-104 enroute to Moscow from Leningrad. A flight attendant attempts to disarm the hijacker, detonating the bomb & killing both. The plane makes an emergency landing in Leningrad.

May 18 • A hijacker with a bomb demands that an Aeroflot flight from Irkutsk to Chita be diverted to China. The bomb detonates, crashing the plane & killing all 82 people on board.

June 10 • In a heist planned by Nepalese politician Girija Koirala, 3 armed men force a Royal Nepalese Airlines plane to land, making off with 3 million Indian rupees which were being transported.

May 30 • Two armed former Paraguayan football players dressed as guerillas hijack flight SAM Colombia HK-1274 with 84 passengers onboard between Pereira and Medellin. They demand $200,000, but escape during a landing in Argentina.

July 20 • Japan Airlines flight 404 between Amsterdam and Tokyo is hijacked by 5 Japanese & Palestinian terrorists on behalf of the PLO. One hijacker is killed when a grenade detonates. The crew and 123 passengers are released in Libya, and the remaining hijackers escape.

October 18 • Danielle Cravenne, the wife of a French film producer, is shot and killed by a police sniper when she attempts to hijack a flight between Paris and Nice.

November 25 • Three Arab men hijack a KLM flight over Iraq on an Amsterdam to Tokyo flight with 247 passengers onboard. After threatening to blow up the plane, most of the passengers are released unharmed in Malta and the remainder in Dubai.

December 17 • After firebombing a terminal in Rome, killing 30, five gunmen shoot a police officer and commandeer Lufthansa flight 303. After stops in Athens and Damascus, the plane lands in Kuwait, where the terrorists are given "free passage" to escape, along with their weapons.

ON JANUARY 5, 1973, the Federal Aviation Administration (FAA) implements emergency rules requiring all passengers and their carry-on baggage to be screened.

ARAB GUERRILLAS KILL 31 IN ROME DURING ATTACK ON U.S. AIRLINER, TAKE HOSTAGES AND GO TO ATHENS

The Rome-Fiumicino International Airport Attack

In a landmark decision, the U.S. Supreme Court under Chief Justice Warren Burger strikes down federal and state abortion laws when it rules that the Constitution confers the right of a woman to abortion. The case of *Roe v. Wade* was brought by a Texas woman who desired an abortion but lived in a state where the procedure was illegal. In a 7-2 decision, the court cites the 14th Amendment which, among other things, grants a citizen's right to privacy. In 2022, the Supreme Court will overturn *Roe v. Wade*, ruling that the Constitution does not confer the right to abortion.

The first issue of ***Playgirl*** is published in June. The "magazine for women" features photos of nude & near-naked men.

And publisher Richard Stolley releases the first test issue of ***People*** magazine, featuring Richard Burton and Elizabeth Taylor on the cover. It is a massive hit, leading to an official launch. *People* will become the most profitable magazine in the U.S., with a readership of 2.35 million.

The runaway bestselling ***Dr. Atkins Diet Revolution*** motivates many to embark on the low-carbohydrate fad diet. The program is not without its critics, who claim it is unbalanced and promtes unlimited consumption of protein & saturated fats.

Over 200 Ogala Lakota and American Indian Movement activists seize Wounded Knee, South Dakota on the Pine Ridge Indian Reservation on February 27th. Their occupation of the town is in protest of the U.S. government's failure to fulfill treaties with Native Americans. The action draws widespread media attention, as well as endorsements from prominent public figures and entertainers, including Johnny Cash, Marlon Brando and Jane Fonda. As the occupation drags on, federal agents cut power, water and food supplies to Wounded Knee.

Following exchanges of gunfire resulting in fatalities and injuries, a disarmament agreement is negotiated 71 days after the beginning of the Siege of Wounded Knee.

1973 BEAUTY QUEENS

MISS WORLD
Marjorie Wallace
(USA)

MISS AMERICA
Terry Meeuwsen
(Wisconsin)

MISS UNIVERSE
Margie Moran
(Philippines)

Wallace

Meeuwsen

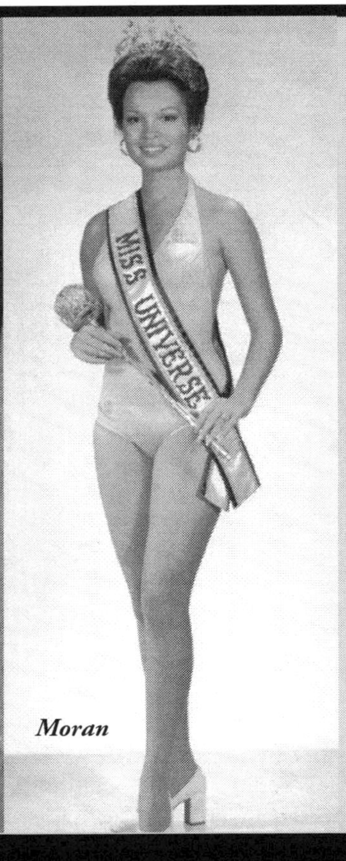

Moran

The world population *increases by nearly 2% to* 3.92 billion *in 1973. The* U.S. population *climbs to almost* 212 million.

Researchers at the **Menlo Park Stanford Research Institute (SRI)** conduct tests in telepathic communication with renowned Israeli psychic **Uri Geller**. Initially skeptical, some of the scientists are impressed with Geller's demonstrations of ESP and psychokinesis (the ability to move objects without touching them).

The researchers are quickly brought back to reality by professional magician and skeptic **James Randi**, who debunks Geller's claims and reveals the fraud by duplicating each of the feats using sleight of hand, audience distraction and other magician's tricks.

Geller

Randi

Passings

ALFRED CARL FULLER, 88 - Founder of Fuller Brush Co.

MAX YASGUR, 53 - dairy farmer who opened his 600-acre New York farm to the Woodstock music festival.

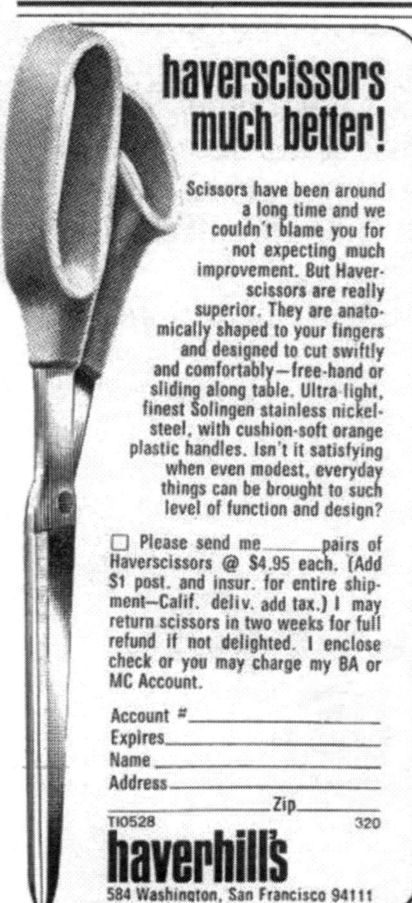

DISASTERS

Michoacan

The Luhuo Earthquake

February 6 -- A magnitude 7.4 earthquake in the Sichuan Province of China kills over 2,200 people. Nearly 16,000 homes along the rupture are destroyed while nearly 3,000 buildings are heavily damaged. 50 landslides are triggered in the Xianshui River valley.

A **7.5 magnitude earthquake** shatters **Michoacan, Mexico**, killing **56 people** on January 30th.

Mississippi flood

In the winter of 1972-1973, heavy rains saturate the **Ohio Valley** and the lower **Missippi Valley**, leading to catastrophic flooding in the lower Missippi River. Near Memphis, the river stays above flood stage for 63 days, and 107 days upstream. 33 people are killed and damage is assessed at $253 million.

Lofthouse Colliery mine

January 23 – **Volcanic cone Eldfell** on the Icelandic island Heimaey erupts.

March 21 – **Seven miners are and killed** when a mine floods in Great Britain's Lofthouse Colliery disaster.

June 17 – **Two of four men die** when the submersible craft *Johnson Sea Link* becomes entangled in wreckage off Key West, Florida.

July 5 - **A BLEVE (Boiling Liquid Expanding Vapor Explosion)** in Kingman, Arizona, kills 11 firefighters.

August 2 – **51 people are killed** in a fire at Summerland amusement park in the UK's Isle of Man.

October 15 – **Typhoon Ruth** hits Luzon, Philippines, killing 27 people and causing $5 million in damage.

November 29 – **104 people are killed** in a fire at Taiyo department store in Kumamoto, Japan.

Taiyo department store fire

AIRLINE DISASTERS

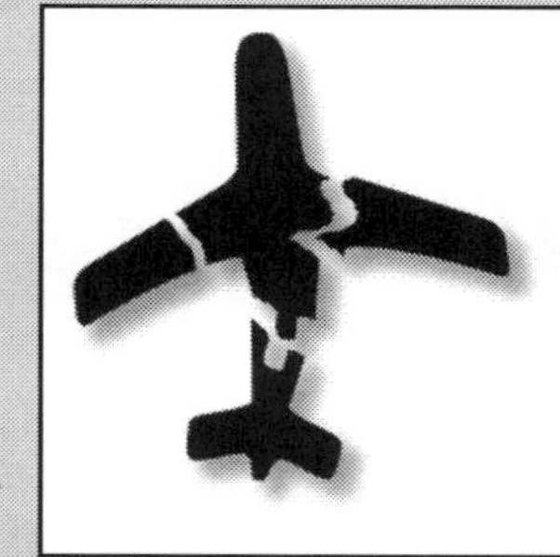

January 22 – A Royal Jordanian Boeing 707 flight from Jeddah crashes in Kano, Nigeria, killing 176 people.

February 21 – Libyan Arab Airlines Flight 114 (Boeing 727), suspected of being an enemy military plane, is shot down by Israeli fighter aircraft over the Sinai Desert. Only 5 of 113 passengers survive.

June 3 – A Tupolev Tu-144 crashes at the Paris air show, killing 15.

June 26 – Nine are killed in the explosion of a Cosmos 3-M rocket at Plesetsk Cosmodrome, Russia.

July 11 – Varig Flight 820 crashes near Orly, France. 123 passengers and crew are killed.

July 31 – Delta Air Lines DC-9 Flight 173 lands short of the runway at Boston's Logan Airport, striking a sea wall. All 83 passengers and 6 crew members are killed.

Flight 173 Logan Airport

1973 ADVERTISEMENT

Calculators, as the saying goes, are the perfect Christmas gift.

But what the saying doesn't say is that some calculators are more perfect than others.

Which brings us to the Bowmar Brains. America's No. 1 selling line of personal calculators.

In 1971, we at Bowmar developed the technology that's responsible for the personal calculator as we know and love it today.

With this head-start, it's no wonder we're out-distancing all the johnnies-come-lately.

We have a broader and fuller line than anyone else has. It's 12 models full. And it has more floating decimals, more percentage keys, more automatic constants, more memories and more 8, 10 and 12 digit read-outs.

Our prices start at $59.95 and go up from there. A small price to pay for the joy and satisfaction of knowing you've given a Brain for Christmas.

The Bowmar Brains

America's No. 1 selling line of personal calculators.

What's New

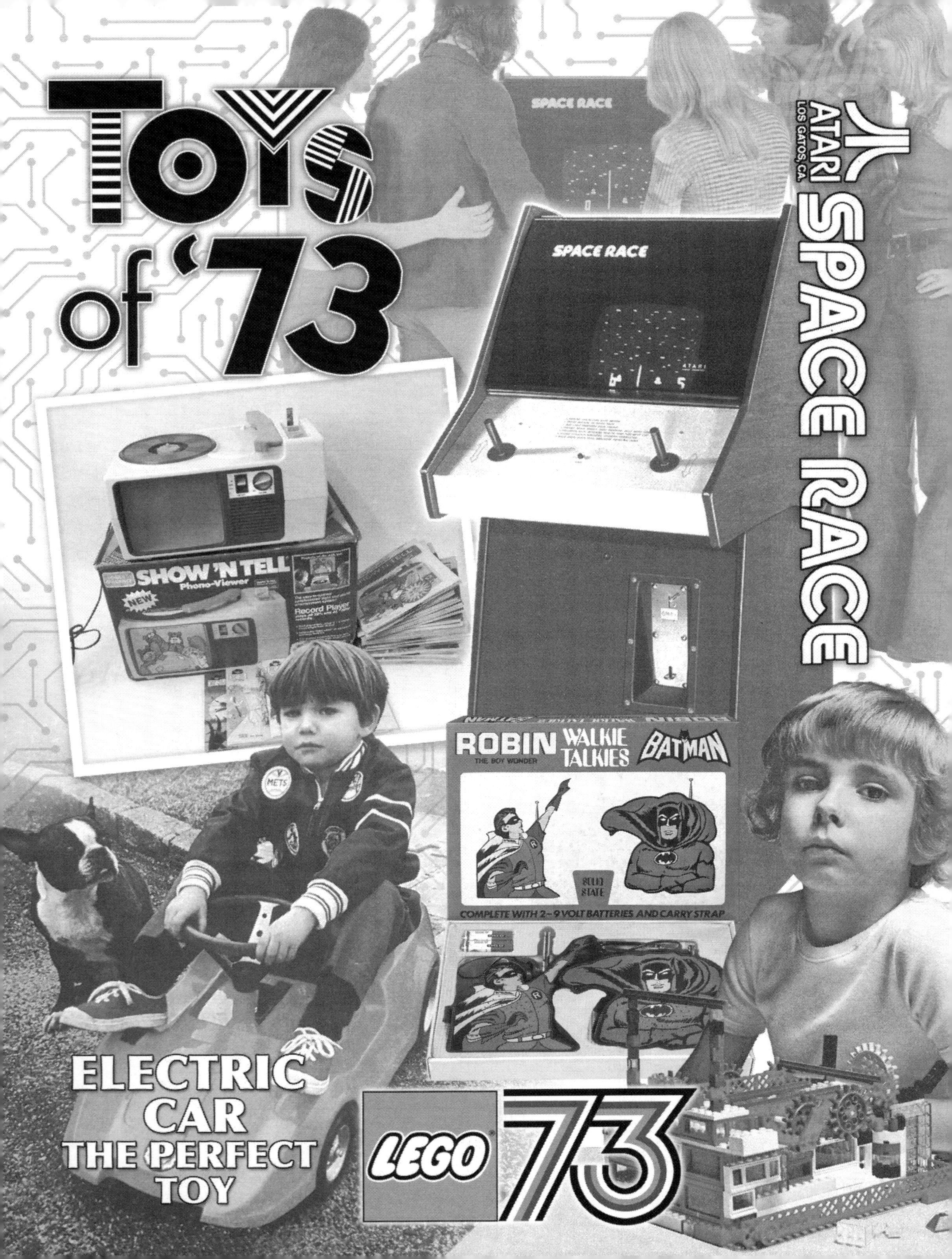
TOYS of '73
SPACE RACE
ATARI
LOS GATOS, CA.
SPACE RACE
SPACE RACE
SHOW 'N TELL
Phono-Viewer
NEW
Record Player
METS
ROBIN
THE BOY WONDER
WALKIE TALKIES
BATMAN
SOLID STATE
COMPLETE WITH 2–9 VOLT BATTERIES AND CARRY STRAP
ELECTRIC
CAR
THE PERFECT
TOY
LEGO
73

New PRODUCTS And INVENTIONS

April 3

THE FIRST-EVER CELL PHONE CALL

Motorola's cell phone featured in *Popular Science*.

Martin Cooper

Standing on Sixth Avenue, between 53rd and 54th streets, **Motorola** engineer **Martin Cooper** makes the very first public call on the DynaTAC 8000X, the first handheld portable cell phone. The first call is to Dr. Joel S. Engel of Bell Labs, his counterpart in the cellular phone race.

Shaped like a brick, it weighs about 2.4 pounds with a price tag of $4,000. Maximum talk-time is around 30 minutes, requiring 10 hours of charge time.

JANUARY 1973

Schoolhouse Rock! debuts as a series of animated shorts with **Multiplication Rock** as the first of the series. The songs, written by **Bob Dorough** are performed by Dorough, **Grady Tate** and **Blossom Dearie**. A soundtrack album is released by Capitol Records.

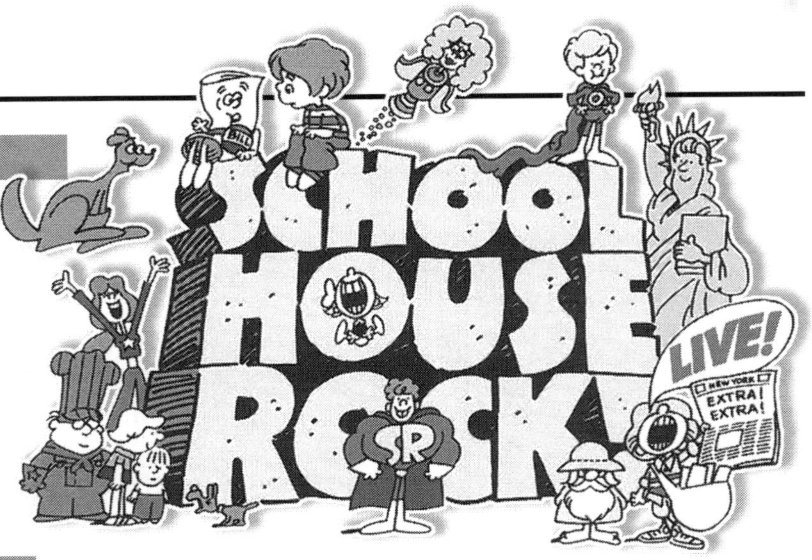

JANUARY 1973

Carl Sontheimer unveils his **Cuisinart**, a name he borrowed from a line of fancy French pots and pans. With a steep retail price of $175, Cuisinart targets the well-heeled home cooks and fans of French Cooking shows. The food processor is sold through Williams-Sonoma and Bloomingdales.

SEPTEMBER 1973

RADIO-ELECTRONICS magazine features the **TV Typewriter**, a predecessor to the personal computer that displays alphanumeric information when connected to an ordinary television set.

NEW BRANDS .... NEW COMPANIES

MEN'S WEARHOUSE®
"You're going to like the way you look; I guarantee it."

golden corral®
Buffet & Grill

AUTOMOBILE TRENDS

Chevrolet's Monte Carlo, with its' European style comfort and handling, sells nearly a quarter-million in 1973, setting a new Chevrolet sales record.

MUSCLE CAR

Pontiac Trans Am 455 SD 455 V-8

With 290 horsepower, Pontiac forges ahead with excitement in the 1973 Muscle Car arena.

A MILESTONE! In October, with the oil crisis gripping the country, a handful of engineers, auto executives and EPA officials meet for the first Symposium on Low Pollution Power at the Ann Arbor Marriott Motor Inn — in the parking lot. The exhibit offers low-emission prototypes for the future of the car industry.

SUNDANCER developed by battery giant, Exide

GM Urban Electric car hooked up for curb-side charge

Lear Steam Bus

NEWS The Latest
Death
NATIONAL LAMPOON
JAN.1973, THE HUMOR MAGAZINE 75 CENTS
If You Don't Buy This Magazine
Newsweek
February 26, 1973
50 cents
HOME AT LAST!
Esquire
MAY 1973
photoplay
FILM MONTHLY
FEBRUARY 1974
20p
NEWMAN & REDFORD in THE STING
Special feature inside
THE PETER (Columbo) FALK STORY
Courage and the Constitution by Richard Goodwin
ROLLING STONE
THE PUBIC HAIR PAPERS & HUGH HEFNER
Ringo Reconvenes the Beatles;
Townshend Returns to the Mod
EBONY
SUICIDE: A Growing Menace To Black Women
Adoption Trends: The Fight For Black Babies
HANK AARON: Catching Up With 'The Babe'
LIFE
SPECIAL REPORT
1973
The year in pictures
ENTERTAINMENT FOR MEN
APRIL 1973 • ONE DOLLAR
PLAYBOY
SPECIAL
MULTINATIONAL CORPORATIONS IN A CHANGING ENVIRONMENT
A Special Report
EQUITY FUNDING: ANATOMY OF A SCANDAL
THE MYSTERIOUS MICHELE SINDONA
FORTUNE
August 1973
COSMOPOLITAN

MAGAZINES
America's Only Rock 'n' Roll Magazine
Creem
ALVIN LEE THE INVULNERABLE BULLOCK!
GARY GLITTER ANDROID SUPERSTAR!
OH WOW!
BOY HOWDY!
GASP!
AND NOW SPIDER-MAN AND THE MARVEL COMICS GROUP!
BATTLING BELLA IS BACK!
Ms.
The Wedding Night & Other Rituals
A Domestic Worker Finally Tells All
Sports Illust
PHILADELPHIA MIRACLE MAN STEVE CARLTON
WHO KNOWS WHAT EVIL LURKS IN THE HEARTS OF MEN?
20¢
The Shadow
1st DC ISSUE
MARVEL COMICS GROUP
MAD
LEGION OF SUPER-HEROES
HELP! SUPERBOY'S GONE MAD!
16 MAGAZINE
SEX-Y DO YOU DA
ENTER THE WORLD OF DANGER, DRAMA AND DEATH!
NIGHT NURSE
I'LL LOSE THE MAN I LOVE FOREVER!
LINDA, STOP! YOU DON'T KNOW WHAT
'74 MUSTANG-WHAT HAPP
MOTOR TREND
PRO-CON FORUM No-Fault Insu
15 NEW MONTHLY FEATU
WIN C
ANNOUNCING MOTOR TREND'S HALL OF FAME
'74 VEGA
NASCAR REPORT
Oct. 15, 1973
Price 50 ce
THE NEW YORKE
down beat
jazz-blues-rock
QUINCY JONES
ORNETTE COLEMAN
GERRY NIEWOOD
LEROY JENKINS
ALVIN QUEEN
WAR

1973 ADVERTISEMENT

PEPPERONI AND SONY.®

A screen almost the size of a kid's baseball glove. 7 diagonal inches.

A playing time of over 4 hours without recharging. That's a ballgame and a Western.

A neat 15-lb. set. With space for the optional batteries right inside.

Sony built it especially for outdoor pleasures like hot dogs or pepperoni.

No baloney.

Science

SPACE IS THE PLACE

May 14 **The** United States launches the first unmanned space station, **Skylab 1**.

The launch from the NASA Kennedy Space Center is a success, though the space station sustains some damage to it's solar array.

SPACE

Three successive crews of astronauts will dock with the station and carry out repairs, observe the human body in the outer space environment, study the Sun in detail, and pioneer Earth-resourced observations.

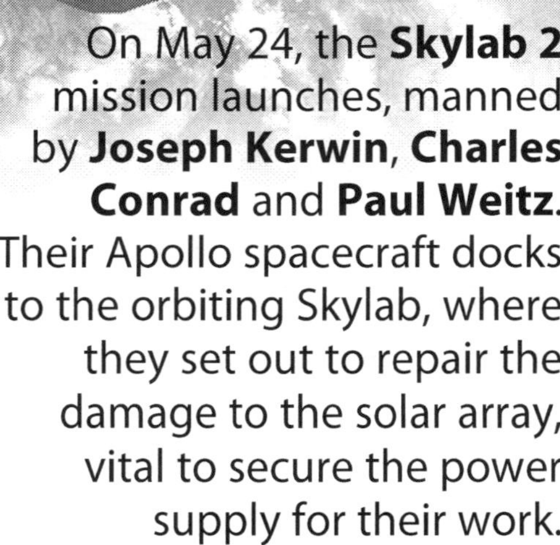

(L. to R.) Joseph Kerwin, Charles Conrad and Paul Weitz

On May 24, the **Skylab 2** mission launches, manned by **Joseph Kerwin**, **Charles Conrad** and **Paul Weitz**. Their Apollo spacecraft docks to the orbiting Skylab, where they set out to repair the damage to the solar array, vital to secure the power supply for their work.

November 3: The Mariner 10 robotic space probe is launched, the first probe to study the planet Mercury

Jan 9: Luna 21 launches, to the Moon

Apr 5: Pioneer 11 launches to Jupiter

Dec 3: Pioneer 10 passes Jupiter (1st fly-by of an outer planet)

Dec 4: Pioneer 10 reaches Jupiter

April 20: Canada's ANIK A2 becomes the first commercial satellite in orbit

USSR

Feb 15: USSR launches Prognoz 3 to study the Sun (589 / 200,300 km)

Jul 25: USSR launches Mars 5

Dec 18: USSR launches Soyuz 13 into Earth orbit for 8 days

Dec 30: 1st picture of a comet from space (Comet Kohoutek-Skylab)

1973

On July 28, the **Skylab 3** mission launches, manned by **Alan Bean**, **Owen K. Garriott** and **Jack Lousma**. They set a new record for the longest spaceflight — 59 days.

(L. to R.) Owen K. Garriott, Jack Lousma and Alan Bean

In November, the **Skylab 4** mission is launched, manned by **Gerald P. Carr**, **William R. Pogue** and **Edward G. Gibson**. One important lesson learned is that the astronauts need more exercise in order to keep their leg muscles strong. The crew sets up makeshift treadmills and bungee supported exercises to support their fitness.

(L. to R.) Gerald P. Carr, Edward G. Gibson and William R. Pogue

America's recycling program in space.

United Technology Center, an aerospace contractor, claims that almost everything used in the space program is and will be recyclable. The giant solid rocket that boosts shuttles into space can land back on earth. The orbiters can be utilized time and time again. Shuttles will take scientists and specialists to the space station for various tasks. The possible studies in space by scientists, agricultural experts and meteorologists will benefit earth, forecasting weather and general conditions on the ground and in the atmosphere – all from space.The recycling program will save millions of dollars, earth's resources and minimize space waste.

United Technology Center

DIVISION OF UNITED AIRCRAFT CORPORATION

PHYSIOLOGY AND MEDICAL ADVANCES

HOW WE SEE BODIES

Paul Lauterbur produces the first resonance image (MRI), via a nuclear magnetic resonance imaging system. It furthers the work of Raymond Damadian's NMR principle.

"Monoclonal antibodies" are successfully produced by **Jerrold Schwaber** and **Edward Cohen**, utilizing human-mouse hybrid cells.

ROAD TO BUILDING IMMUNITY:
Ralph Steinman and **Zanvil Cohn** discover an unusual looking population of cells with an ability to activate naïve T-cells. Dubbed "dendritic cells," these cells are now known as the primary instigators of adaptive immunity.

"Norrmalmstorgssyndromet"

Stockholm Syndrome is coined by **Nils Bejerot.** It describes victim's sympathy with oppressors, as was observed at the bank robbery in Stockholm, Sweden in August. During the six-day standoff with police, the captive bank employees became sympathetic toward the bank robbers. Years later, lawyer **F. Lee Bailey** would use "Stockholm Syndrome" as a defense for **Patricia Hearst's** participation in a Symbionese Liberation Army bank robbery.

December 15: **The American Psychiatric Association declares that "homosexuality per se" is not a mental disorder.**

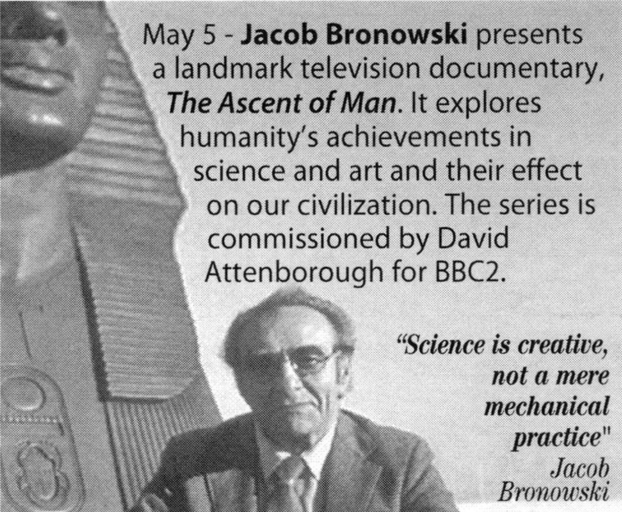

May 5 - **Jacob Bronowski** presents a landmark television documentary, ***The Ascent of Man***. It explores humanity's achievements in science and art and their effect on our civilization. The series is commissioned by David Attenborough for BBC2.

"Science is creative, not a mere mechanical practice"
Jacob Bronowski

FLOURIDE

June 22: The Dutch High Council halts the addition of fluoride to drinking water.

The EMS Services Development Act of 1973 designates the Department of Health, Education and Welfare as the lead Emergency Medical Services agency within the U.S. federal government.

• • • DEATH • • •

March 14 - **Howard H. Aiken** was a major figure of the early digital era, known for his first machine, the IBM Automatic Sequence Controlled Calculator, a forerunner of the modern electronic digital computer.

July 11 - **Laurens Hammond** American engineer and inventor of the Hammond organ, the Hammond clock and the first polyphonic musical synthesizer (Novachord). During WWII, he helped design guided missile controls and was awarded patents for infrared devices for bomb guidance.

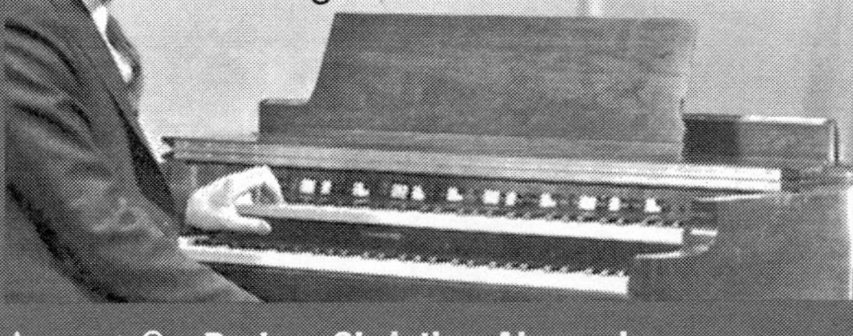

August 9 - **Preben Christian Alexander von Magnus** Danish virologist – first to identify the monkey pox virus.

August 12 - **Walter Rudolf Hess** Swiss physiologist, recipient of the 1949 Nobel Prize in Physiology/Medicine for mapping the area of the brain involved in the control of internal organs.

August 16 - **Selman Abraham Waksman** Biochemist and microbiologist. His studies of soil microbes led to the discovery of streptomycin, revolutionizing the treatment of tuberculosis. He coined the word "antibiotics."

THE TURING AWARD

Charles W. Backman

Named for British mathematician Alan Turing, it is an annual prize given since 1966 to an individual for major contributions to the computer field.

CHARLES W. BACKMAN receives the Turing Award from the Association for Computing Machinery for "his outstanding contributions to database technology."

MOUSE TRACKING

March 1, 1973, engineers at Xerox Palo Alto Research Center (PARC) create a revolutionary computer called the Xerox Alto that pioneers the mouse-based graphical user interface (GUI), bitmap-ped graphics, local networking, laser printing, networked computer gaming, and much more – setting the standard for personal computing.

Scientist Butler Lampson first proposed the Alto in a December 19, 1972 memorandum to the Xerox Corporation.

BIRTHS

Future **Google** Co-Founders
Lawrence (Larry) Page / March 26
Sergey Brin / August 21

Neam "Nim" Chimpsky
A chimpanzee born November 19th will become a study subject of animal language acquisition at Columbia University in a project led by Herbert S. Terrace. The chimp's name is a play on MIT linguist, Noam Chomsky.

NOBEL PRIZE

The Nobel Prizes, according to Alfred Nobel's will of 1895, are awarded to those who have conferred the greatest benefit to humankind.

PHYSIOLOGY OR MEDICINE:

Nobel Prize shared in Physiology or Medicine for their discoveries of animal behavior patterns as groups and as individuals.

NIKOLAAS TINBERGEN (Dutch biologist and ornithologist) studied bee-killer wasps and their use of landmarks to navigate.

KAROL VON FRISCH (German-Austrian ethologist) discovered the "dance" of the honeybees, demonstrating that worker bees communicate information to co-workers.

KONRAD LORENZ (Austrian zoologist, ethologist and ornithologist) is famous for studies of animal behavior.

Nikolaas Tinbergen on a visit with Konrad Lorenz

PHYSICS:

The 1973 Nobel Prize in Physics, shared for their work in electron tunneling in semiconductor materials.

LEO ESAKI (Japanese Physicist)

IVAR GIAEVER (Norwegian-American Engineer and Physicist)

BRIAN DAVID JOSEPHSON (Welsh Physicist)

Leo Esaki

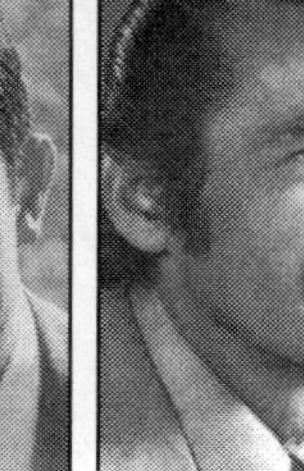
Ivar Giaever

Brian David Josephson

1973 ADVERTISEMENT

Ever since the day we began making autos 40 years ago Toyota has faced one fact we can never get around. Our home country is one of the most densely populated in the world. So right from the start we've had to meet the consumers' demand for a good small car.

Our philosophy has remained the same to the present day. Everything we have goes into satisfying the world's need for a safe, reliable, well built small car. And the way we've been accepted in over a hundred and twenty countries tells us we've been on the right track all along.

In the days to come Toyota plans to concentrate its extensive research and development facilities on solving the problems we are all aware of. Because if we don't use yesterday's experience to overcome today's difficulties no one can have a decent tomorrow.

TOYOTA

BUSINESS

U.S. Federal Budget	$246.3B
Inflation Rate	7.6%
Unemployment	5.6%

1973
Average Movie Ticket Price: $1.77
Inflation Adjusted: $9.94

Top-Grossing Movie of the Year:
The Exorcist

First-Class Stamp Holds Steady at 8¢.

On January 26, USPS issues the **Love Stamp**, bearing a design by **Robert Indiana.**

Federal Minimum Wage
$1.60/hour

Median Annual U.S. Family Income $12,050

Black families in the U.S. $7,270
The income for women: ± $5,797

Average Annual U.S. Earnings for:

Professional	$18,348
Farmers	$18,494
Farm Labor	$5,853
Managers/Admin	$18,494
Clerical	$12,314
Sales	$15,591
Craftsmen	$13,785
Housekeepers	$4,282
Service Workers	$10,059
Laborers	$10,463
Teachers	$10,770

California Certified Organic Farmers (CCOF) is founded in Santa Cruz, California

S•L•O•W•I•N•G THE SPEED LIMIT

California lowers the speed limit from 75 to 65 mph, while Texas, in late May, lowers theirs statewide to 55 mph.

LINES AT THE GAS STATIONS

The U.S. Department of Energy reports the average price for a gallon of gasoline is 39 cents. There are long lines and panic buying at the pumps as Americans are shocked to see gas rationing and shortages.

THE FEDERAL BUDGET DOLLAR

Fiscal Year 1973 Estimate

Where it comes from...

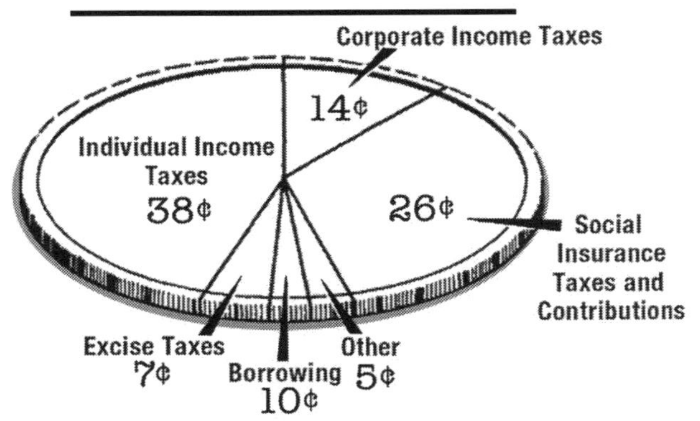

Where it goes...

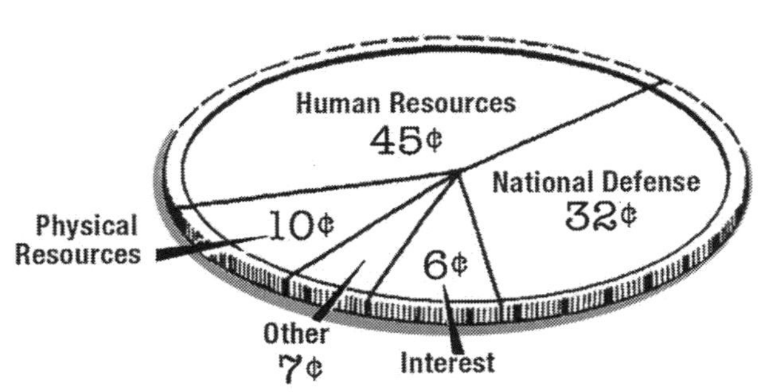

U.S. unemployment: **5.6%** | the average family income: **$12,900** | minimum hourly wage: **$1.60**
new house cost: **$32,500** | average price for a gallon of gas: **38.5¢** | an ounce of gold **$106.48**

AVERAGE COST OF A **NEW HOUSE 1973**

$32,500.00

AVERAGE MONTHLY RENT

$191.00

AVERAGE TUITION AT A **FOUR-YEAR PUBLIC COLLEGE**

$358

Least-Expensive '73 Car

Introducing the 1973 Beetle:

Re-introducing the 1972 price: $1999.*

Most-Expensive '73 Cars

Mercedes-Benz 450 Series SLC Coupe

$15,094

Porsche 911 S Targa

$10,555

STOCKS

1973 Dow Jones Industrial Average

Average Closing Price: **850** .... Year High: **1051** .... Year Low: **788**

STOCK MARKET CRASH!

Between January 11 and December 6, the Dow Jones Industrial Average suffers one of it's worst markets, losing over 45% of it's value. Rising gas prices, the embargo on OPEC oil and spending on the Viet Nam war leads the economy into recession.

The Dow in the 1970s

★ TOP 10 RANKED BUSINESSES IN THE DOW ★

RANK	COMPANY	REVENUES ($millions)	PROFITS ($ millions)
1	General Motors	30,435.2	2,162.8
2	Exxon Mobil	20,309.8	1,531.8
3	Ford Motor	20,194.4	870.0
4	General Electric	10,239.5	530.0
5	Chrysler	9,759.2	220.5
6	IBM	9,532.6	1,279.3
7	Mobil	9,166.3	543.2
8	Texaco	8,693.0	889.9
9	ITT Industries	8,556.8	483.3
10	AT&T Technologies	6,551.2	282.9

Sears
Perma-Prest® Short-Sleeve Dress Shirts
4 for $10
Perma-Prest® for Easy Care
Exclusive C-band® Comfort Collar
Tapered and Trim Styling
K mart KM 200, 2 GLASS BELTS + 2 POLYESTER CORDS
15.00
K mart KM 20, 4-FULL-PLY NYLON CORD
Blackwalls
9.88
K mart KM 300, 4 PLIES POLYESTER CORD + 2 FIBERGLASS BELTS
23.00
Bring a Dole Banana and Save!
SPLIT THE PRICE OF A SPLIT
at DAIRY QUEEN*
Offer good Oct. 1-7
Dairy Queen
"Let's all go to the DAIRY QUEEN."
Washington's Birthday Special From the Colonel
FREE CHERRY PIE
Free Cherry Pie
with this coupon and a purchase of:
Barrel or Family Pack
CLIP COUPON
Kentucky Fried Chicken
14.88
GRAND
THE CONVENIENT STORE
MEMORIAL DAY
WEEKENDER
STYLES
THE PRICE ¢ ¢
$ $ THAT WAS
Kmart
NEW POCKET-SIZE EVERFLASH CAMERA
$47
INSTANT PICTURE EVERFLASH CAMERA
$53
Exclusive, By Keystone
Save the cost of a flash every time you take a flash picture!
Sears
Sears 8-Track Player and AM/FM Radio
Model 9130
$98
Sears 8-Track Stereo Player with AM/FM Radio
Model 9135
$148
8-Track AM/FM Stereo with Record Changer
Model 9145
YOUR CHOICE: Upright or Canister Vacuum
Kenmore Canister Vac Revolving-Brush Upright
USDA INSPECTED • GOLD SEAL QUALITY BEEF
Stew Beef
BONELESS
$1.08 lb.
Roast
Pork Shoulder Steak
Pork Butt Roast
Pork Spare Ribs
Smoked Picnics
Sliced & Tied Smoked Picnics
DELICATESSEN SAVINGS
Sears
SAVE $2 on Chukka Boots for the Family!
Chukka Boots and Ladies' Casuals
9.97 pair
6.97 pair
5.97 pair
4.97 pair
8.97 pair
Ask About Sears Convenient Credit Plans

She'll enjoy dinner at Ponderosa. You will too. Hearty steak. Baked Idaho potato. Tossed green salad and roll. And even a sidekick won't kick at the price.

$1.99 SIRLOIN STEAK DINNER

PONDEROSA STEAK HOUSE

Very little wampum for great steak. Served with baked Idaho potato, tossed green salad and roll. Take the tribe tonight. Or tomorrow. It'll be a feather in your cap.

$1.99 SIRLOIN STEAK DINNER

PONDEROSA STEAK HOUSE

WAL-MART Discount City

SATISFACTION GUARANTEED

Sale Ends Sat. 12-1-73

Bus Service Daily to Wal-Mart

OPEN DAILY TILL 10 P.M. THRU CHRISTMAS

WE ALWAYS SELL FOR LESS EVERYDAY

Suggestions from Santa

Crock Pot $9.97

BAKER-BROILER $26.97

CORN POPPER $8.87

Chip and Dip Salad Set $1.67

In Keeper

Ford Tractor $4.26

Mr. Bim Jr.

Shick Hot Lather Machine $8.87

Instamatic® 10 Outfit $13.97

Square Shooter 2 $16.97

SPICE RACK $1.57

SNACK SET $1.57

Knuckle Busters $4.97

Pursuit $4.96

Super Dog Hot Roadster

Super Dog Flying Machine $1.86

$1.16

SHOTGUN SHELLS $1.67

$2.27

Tree Balls

Miniature Tree Lights

Holiday Jumbo Log Gift Wrap

Tree Lites

TOYS "R" US

the CHILDREN'S Bargain Town

"SCARCELY" SOMETHING TO "BOO" ABOUT: BIG SELECTIONS! LOW PRICES!

COLLEGEVILLE BARBIE BRIDE COSTUME — FLAME RETARDANT — Sizes S,M,L for children — 3.48 OUR PRICE

SPIDER-MAN COSTUME — FLAME RETARDANT — Sizes S,M,L for children — 3.78 OUR PRICE

Herman Iskin COWBOY PLAYSUIT — Washable, use for every-day play! — Sizes S,M,L for children — 12.97 OUR PRICE

ALL COLLEGEVILLE AT DISCOUNTS — ALL COOPER AT BIG DISCOUNTS — ALL ISKIN AT BIG DISCOUNTS

BLAND CHARNAS TINY TOT COSTUME ASSORTMENT — FLAME RETARDANT — 1.18 OUR PRICE

YODA COSTUME — FLAME RETARDANT — Sizes S,M,L for children — 3.87 OUR PRICE

COLLEGEVILLE PEANUTS CHARACTERS COSTUME ASSORTMENT — FLAME RETARDANT — Sizes S,M,L for children — 3.48 OUR PRICE

TRICK OR TREAT

DON POST — DEVIL MONSTER MASK — 6.97

COLLEGEVILLE — HOBO — 38¢

NON-TOXIC PLAY BLOOD — 58¢

PARTY NAPKINS

GUARANTEED! PANTRY PRIDE OFFERS THE

LOWEST PRICES

THAT ARE ADVERTISED EVERY WEEK!

Pantry Pride

LOOK FOR THE TEMPORARY PRICE REDUCTIONS... THEY SAVE YOU EVEN MORE THAN DISCOUNT PRICES!

USDA INSPECTED • GOLD SEAL QUALITY BEEF

Chuck Roast — 78¢ lb.

Boneless Chuck Roast

Shoulder Clod

Seven-Bone Roast

Bone Roast

Family Steak

USDA INSPECTED • GOLD SEAL QUALITY BEEF

Stew Beef — BONELESS — $1.08 lb.

Boneless Chuck Steaks — 98¢

Bone Swiss Steak — 98¢

Fresh Water Smelts — 59¢

We're Proud of the Meats We Sell...

UNCONDITIONAL GUARANTEE!

FRESH EASTERN PORK

Pork Roast — 65¢ lb.

Pork Shoulder Steak — 89¢

Pork Butt Roast — 79¢

Pork Spare Ribs — 78¢

Smoked Picnics — 63¢

Sliced & Tied Smoked Picnics — 73¢

DELICATESSEN SAVINGS

This Week's LIQUOR FEATURES

VODKA $3.69 QUART

GIN $3.99

BOURBON $4.88

BRANDY $4.99 QUART

BLENDED WHISKEY $4.99

CANADIAN WHISKY $4.49

SCOTCH $4.99 QUART

HOT OFFER 31

We'll buy the topping. You buy the ice cream!

We'll give you your choice of a jar of thick, rich and delicious Baskin-Robbins Hot Fudge or Hot Butterscotch topping! Just buy two 24 oz. containers of Baskin-Robbins hand packed ice cream in any one of 31 flavors and take home the topping!

BASKIN-ROBBINS ICE CREAM STORE 31

BUY NOW!

ZENITH

SWIV-L-TILT

TILTS UP OR DOWN 10°—SWIVELS IN COMPLETE 360° CIRCLE!

12" COMPACT TV

DIAGONAL

ONLY $109.95

FOR DELUXE 12" DIAGONAL PORTABLE WITH BUILT-ON "SWIV-L-TILT" BASE

The SOPHISTICATE • E1345

Features Instant Picture & Sound!

TILTS UP — OR DOWN — TURNS ALL AROUND

Now add more enjoyment to your TV viewing with Zenith's convenient "SWIV-L-TILT" Pedestal Base with the look of tomorrow...today! Hurry in today—Supply is limited!

MONTGOMERY WARD

Your Christmas Store

2 DAY SALE

FRIDAY AND SATURDAY NOVEMBER 23 & 24

$5 OFF

THE MOST SKILLED DRIVER WINS WITH OUR FAST 4-CAR SLOTLESS ROADRACE

REG. 34.99 — 29.99

10.88

10.88

'73 OLDS LUXURY SALE

1973 TORONADOS 19 IN STOCK

AS LOW AS $5399

#3-933 Brand-New '73 Toronado Custom; vinyl roof, tinted glass, power seat, power 6-way seat, AM/FM stereo, white sidewalls, more.

SAVE OVER $1300

1973 CUSTOM CRUISERS • 21 IN STOCK

#3-1132 Brand-New 3-Seat Custom Cruiser; air, tinted glass, side moldings, radio, remote mirror, luggage rack, white sidewalls, more. Sticker Price, $5596.40

SAVE $1000

AS LOW AS $459

OLDS. 98's 20 TO CHOOSE

AS LOW

$498

#3-930 Brand-New Olds 98 4-Door Hardtop; full power, including windows, 6-way seat, factory air, tinted glass, AM/FM stereo, white sidewalls and much more. Sticker Price, $6127.80.

Behler Oldsmobile

4040 SPRING GROVE AVE.

MITCHELL OR COLERAIN EXITS — INTERSTATE 75 — 541-1980

59¢

Springfield Bleach

Minneolas — 2-29¢

Papayas — 39¢

Steak Mushrooms — 89¢

Town Onions — 3-39¢

BUNCHES

Golden Bananas — 11¢ lb.

Banana Squash — 10¢

Rutabagas — 10¢

Fresh, Crisp Carrots — 10¢

Fancy, Firm Turnips — 10¢

FOR JUICE • SWEET

Valencia Oranges — 10¢ lb.

SAVE ON FROZEN

Vegetables

Treesweet Orange Juice

Macaroni & Cheese

Snackwiches

Dog Food

Chili with Beans

Wesson

24-OZ. BOTTLE

THERE'S A PANTRY PRIDE NEAR YOU OPEN 24 HOURS

THE 'CRESTWOOD' as shown — with attached garage $19,495 ... or with carport at $18,275 (and your $500.00 Gov't Bonus)

Fully detached homes from $16,745

(and your $500.00 Gov't Bonus)

Some Available For Immediate Occupancy!

plus: At no extra cost: • Arborite Kitchen Counter Top • Built-in Bread Board • Double Stainless Steel Sinks • Kitchen Exhaust Fan • Chrome Bathroom Fixtures • Coloured Ceramic Tile to Ceiling in Bath Tub Enclosure • Double Glazing and Aluminum Screens • Electric Light Fixtures • Door Chime • Fully Sodded Front • Glass-Steel Hot Water Tank (rental) • Paved Roads and Curbs • Storm and Sanitary Sewers • Doubly insulated in Walls and Ceiling • Copper Plumbing.

Finch & Leslie

DIRECTIONS: Bayview to Finch to Leslie and you're there, at Bel Ayr!

NATURAL GAS

HALLmark

DAVIDSON DEVELOPMENTS

Open Daily 10 a.m. to 9 p.m.

1973 ADVERTISEMENT

The Bell Bottom look returns to the fashion playbook along with Clogs and Clunky Shoes for men and women.

Wide Lapels and Wide Ties are a must for men.

& The most important fashion event happens in Versailles, France, where American designers gain worldwide ovations and acclaim.

THE BATTLE OF Versailles

NOVEMBER 28, 1973: AN HISTORIC FASHION EVENT

All the fashion luminaries — the rich, the famous and assorted royalty — are present at the Palace of Versailles to raise money for its restoration. Then, an unintentional Franco-American runway battle ensues: five French designers vs. five American designers. Some say it is the "coming out party" for the Americans — **Oscar de la Renta**, **Stephen Burrows**, **Halston**, **Bill Blass** and **Anne Klein** with her assistant, **Donna Karan** — who steal the show. A stand-out among the lions of the fashion world is a young designer, an American named **Stephen Burrows**. The American designers make fascinating use of jersey — easy to wear, lightweight and sensuously body conscious. With yards and yards of zipperless jersey moving easily down the runway to taped music, the five American designers are the sure winners in the ready-to-wear-for-the-disco set.

Anne Klein

Stephen Burrows

Marc Bohan, Philippe Guibourge, Oscar de la Renta, Halston, Joe Eula and Bill Blass, 1973

While the Fashion Revolution of 1973 will be waged in Versailles...

Rocker DAVID BOWIE challenges the fashion status quo. He has a runway of his own, the concert stage, to showcase his aesthetic — a genderless style from the alter-world.

Bowie's image is realized by his equally creative friends, collaborators and designers:

KANSAI YAMAMOTO

The Japanese designer will be forever linked to David Bowie for his vinyl jumpsuit from the Alladin Sane Tour. His designs become fused with Bowie's invention of Ziggy Stardust.

FREDDIE BURRETTI

"Fred of the East End"

From a tailoring stint on the King's Road, Freddie Burretti proves to be a formidable fashion artist with his friend, David Bowie, the canvas. Burretti created the often quoted and copied, black and white suit which Bowie wore around town. He is also responsible for the "ice-blue satin suit" (David Bowie, Life on Mars, 1972). Bowie's period signature, shock of red-red hair – is influenced by Burretti's girlfriend, Daniella Parmar.

Bill Blass
for Martha
You can bank on Bill Blass
when it comes to the opulent look
He always strikes it rich.
Martha

Neiman Marcus Award for Distinguished Service in The Field of Fashion

HANAE MORI The first Asian designer to influence French haute couture.

MISSONI Recognized for his designs using colorful zig-zag knits in blues, greens, reds and oranges.

JEAN MUIR

RALPH LAUREN

Levi's

Levi Strauss & Company "the single most important American contribution" to the world of fashion. The company goes public.

COTY American Fashion Critics' Award

Stephen Burrows His design of bright garments with "lettuce hem" and curly edges gains immediate attention at the historic fashion show in Versaille.

Calvin Klein His first Coty Award for his classic line with casual flair at a moderate price.

RALPH LAUREN Coty Award for menswear & his "Great Gatsby" costume designs.

HALL of FAME AWARD

Oscar de la Renta His first Coty Award for his casual take on a classic line at a moderate price.

VANITY FAIR BEST DRESSED LIST

Nino Cerruti fashion designer

Hernando Courtwright owner, Beverly Wilshire Hotel

John Galliher socialite, fashion designer

Cristina Ford socialite, second wife of Henry Ford II

Princess Salima Aga Khan child-welfare activist, first wife (begum) of His Highness the Aga Khan

Elsa Peretti jewelry designer

Nancy Reagan Mrs. Ronald Reagan

Anne France Mannheimer (future Annette de la Renta) philanthropist, New York's social queen

Françoise de la Renta & Oscar de la Renta

Christian Dior
FETE DES PERES
LES CRAVATES
ET TOUS LES ACCESSORES
MASCULINS

FASHION FOR HIM: A FLASHBACK

Does this year's look seem familiar? Was it last year? Decades ago? Maybe you've seen the style in an old photo of father or grand-father? Nothing much changes, especially for men's wear. But for all that, this year's fashion encourages men to take chances with what they wear, and doesn't censure them for doing so.

Pants are worn with flares at the ankle, the ties are wide and suit jacket lapels are decidedly wider. The look should be credited to the whimsical tailoring of Tommy Nutter and Freddie Burretti.

Chunky shoes with thick soles and higher heels.

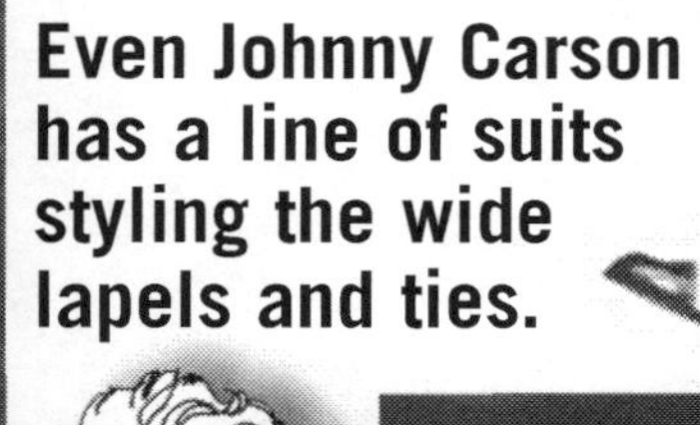

here's johnny

Even Johnny Carson has a line of suits styling the wide lapels and ties.

WIDE BIG TIES &WIDE LAPELS

Simplicity Sewing For Men and Boys Sewing Book

Put on the Ritz
Real Ritz.
A whole collection of
long-blooming perfume
to dive into,
dress up in. To
make you feel
like a million.
RITZ
Charles of the Ritz
© 1973 Charles of the Ritz. Available only
in finest department and specialty stores.

FAMOUS BIRTHS

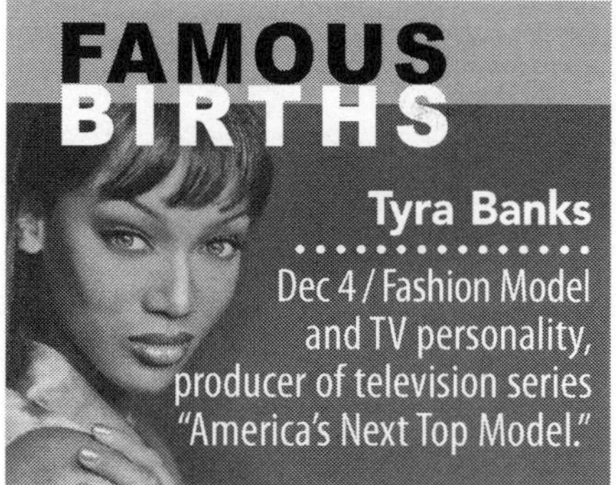

Tyra Banks

Dec 4 / Fashion Model and TV personality, producer of television series "America's Next Top Model."

Fadi Fawaz

May 25 / Hair stylist, photographer. Will work with "The Pussycat Dolls" and Naomi Campbel and known as the last man to see George Michaels alive.

Heidi Klum

Jun 1 / Model Sports Illustrated Swimsuit model (1998) and Victoria's Secret Angel.

Eva Herzigovå

Mar 10 / Model

Phillip Lim

Sep 16 / Fashion Designer

Phoebe Philo

Jan 1 / Fashion Designer

Carolyn Murphy

Aug 11 / Fashion Model

Chandra North

Jul 31 / Fashion Model

BOYs of Zappos!

Tony Hsieh

Dec 12 / co-founder of Zappos

Alfred Lin

Aug 15 /co-founder of Zappos

Nick Swinmurn

Jan 17 / co-founder of Zappos

PASSINGS

Elsa Schiaparelli (designer)
Sept 10, 1890 – Nov. 13, 1973

Schiaparelli arrived in Paris in the late twenties to design gold jewelry while waiting for a chance to break into the world of high fashion. In the 1940s, at her peak, she employed 350 seamstresses and young designers at an establishment on the Place Vendome. One of them, Hubert de Givenchy, became a leading designer In his own right. Her arch-rival, the late Gabrielle (Coco) Chanel referred to her as "that Italian woman who makes dresses." And like Chanel, Schiaparelli lived a mysteriously good life in German-occupied France. American columnist Walter Winchell published a suggestion that Schiaparelli was a spy. But it was gossip, never proven.

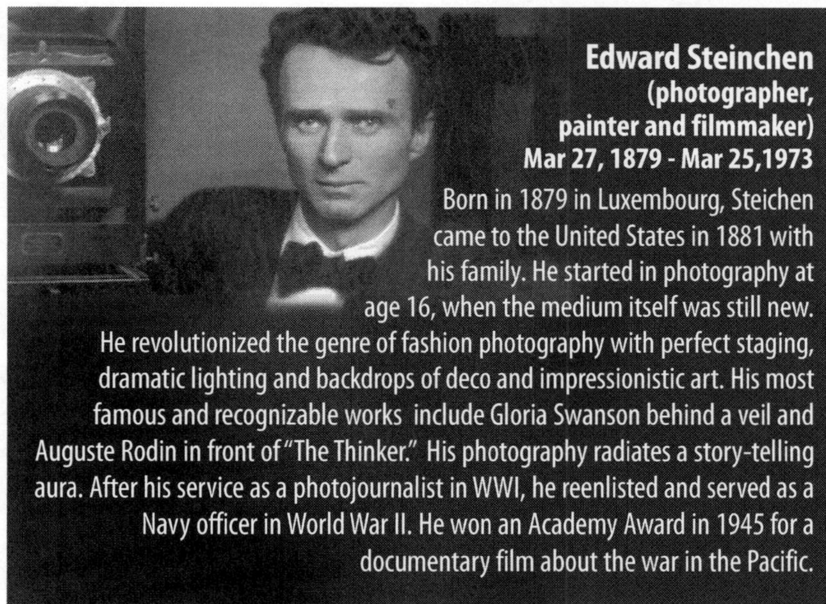

Edward Steinchen (photographer, painter and filmmaker)
Mar 27, 1879 - Mar 25,1973

Born in 1879 in Luxembourg, Steichen came to the United States in 1881 with his family. He started in photography at age 16, when the medium itself was still new. He revolutionized the genre of fashion photography with perfect staging, dramatic lighting and backdrops of deco and impressionistic art. His most famous and recognizable works include Gloria Swanson behind a veil and Auguste Rodin in front of "The Thinker." His photography radiates a story-telling aura. After his service as a photojournalist in WWI, he reenlisted and served as a Navy officer in World War II. He won an Academy Award in 1945 for a documentary film about the war in the Pacific.

Veronica Lake *nee Constance Charlotta Trimble*
(actress) Nov 14, 1922 - Jul 7,1973

Born in Brooklyn, New York, she and her family moved to Beverly Hills in 1938, where her mother enrolled her in acting classes. Her first appearance on screen was for RKO, playing a small role in a 1939 film, "Sorority House." Her visibility was enhanced when a director noticed how her hair always fell to hide her right eye, creating a mysterious look — the "peek-a-boo" hairstyle. Paramount changed her name to Veronica Lake and she garnered fame for her roles in film noirs "This Gun For Hire," "Blue Dahlia" and "Dead Men Don't Wear Plaid."

Susie Maxwell Berning wins her third U.S. Women's Open, playing New Blue Max.

Unlike many women, Susie Maxwell Berning likes to celebrate her birthdays. This year she did it by winning her third U.S. Women's Open Golf Championship, repeating her victories in 1972 and 1968.

Tied for the lead at the end of three rounds, Susie outplayed the field on the final 18 holes at the Country Club of Rochester, finishing strong to win by five strokes at 290 for the tournament. As always, she won playing Dunlop equipment, Maxfli clubs and balls. But this time she did it with a brand new Maxfli ball—the BLUE MAX.

The Blue Max is so new we haven't officially announced it. But it's announcing itself on both tours, with three wins in the last month.

Blue Max is totally new, with a durable, cut-resistant cover of Surlyn,* an exclusive new winding, and a solid, high velocity center. You'll probably play it till you lose it, and that just might happen because Blue Max flies farther than any other durable-cover or solid ball.

They're a little scarce because they're brand new. But ask your golf professional for Blue Max anyway. If he has them, we think you'll agree that it's the most exciting golf ball you've ever played.

BUFFALO, N.Y., TORONTO, ONT.

Sold only through Golf Professionals

*Reg. U.S. Pat. Off. for DuPont's ionomer resin.

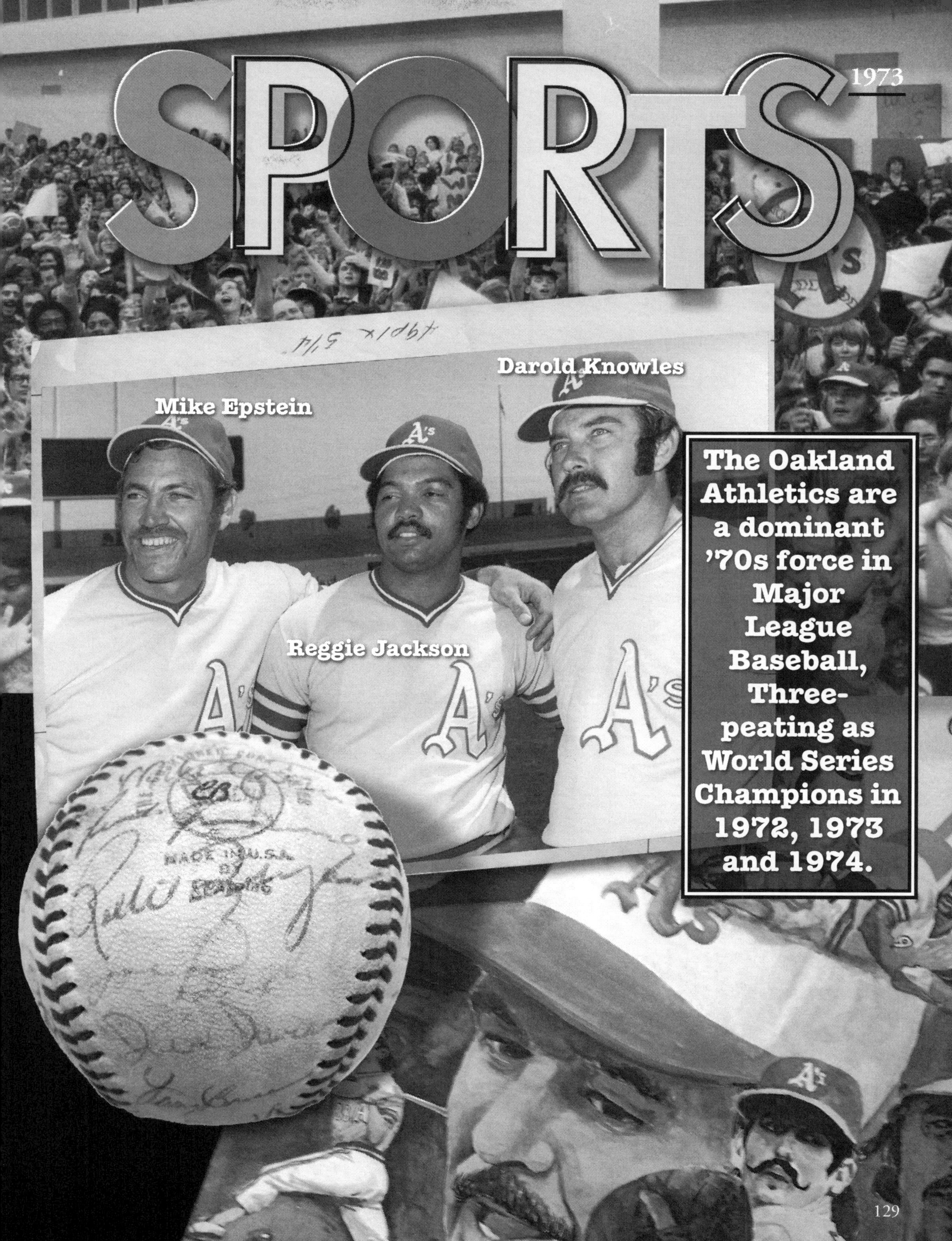

The Oakland Athletics are a dominant '70s force in Major League Baseball, Three-peating as World Series Champions in 1972, 1973 and 1974.

MOST VALUABLE PLAYER

NATIONAL LEAGUE
Pete Rose (Cincinnati Reds)

AMERICAN LEAGUE
Reggie Jackson (Oakland Athletics)

HOME RUN LEADERS

NATIONAL LEAGUE
Willie Stargell (Pittsburgh Pirates, 44)

AMERICAN LEAGUE
Reggie Jackson (Oakland Athletics, 32)

BATTING CHAMPIONS

NATIONAL LEAGUE
Pete Rose (Cincinnati Reds, .338)

AMERICAN LEAGUE
Rod Carew (Minnesota Twins, .350)

ROOKIE OF THE YEAR

NATIONAL LEAGUE
Gary Matthews (San Fran. Giants)

AMERICAN LEAGUE
Al Bumbry (Baltimore Orioles)

Baseball 1973 World Series

OAKLAND ATHLETICS *over* NEW YORK METS 4-3

The 70th edition of the World Series is also the first Series in which all of the weekday games start at night. A's rightfielder and American League homerun leader, **Reggie Jackson**, blasts a two-run homer in game seven, securing the win and snagging the MVP award.

MAJOR LEAGUE ALL-STAR GAME ROYALS STADIUM

On July 24, the **American League** and the **National League** face off at Royals Stadium in Kansas City, MO. The National League emerges victorious, 7-1, with San Francisco Giant **Bobby Bonds** named the MVP.

THE DESIGNATED HITTER RULE

In an effort to enliven the game and boost attendance, the owners of the 24 major-league baseball teams decide to add a tenth man to the lineup in the American League. This means that a pinch hitter will be permitted to bat for a pitcher without the pitcher having to leave the game.

In April, New York Yankee **Ron Blomberg** becomes the first designated hitter in Major League Baseball.

- 1973 BASEBALL - Hall of Fame Inductees

Election to the Hall of Fame follows the system established in 1971. The Baseball Writers' Association of America selects 3 MLB players. The Veterans Committee selects 3. The Negro Leagues Committee selects 2 players.

Roberto Clemente
Right Fielder: Pittsburgh Pirates
1955-1972
(died 1972, aged 38, in plane crash)

Roberto Clemente

Billy Evans
Umpire
At age 22, he became the youngest umpire in MLB history; 3rd umpire elected to Hall of Fame

Monte Irvin
Left Fielder: Newark Eagles
1937-1942, 1945-1956
Played with the Negro League Newark Eagles, as well as the New York Giants and the Chicago Cubs.

"Long George" Kelly
First Baseman: New York Giants
1915-1917, 1919-1930, 1932

Warren Spahn
Pitcher: Milwaukee Braves
1942, 1946-1965
Also played for the New York Mets & the San Francisco Giants

Mickey Welch
Pitcher: New York Giants
1880-1892

Secretariat: HORSE of the YEAR

Secretariat, also known as, **Big Red**, is regarded as one of the greatest thoroughbred race horses of all time. In 1973, he becomes the ninth Triple Crown winner, the first Triple Crown winner in 25 years, and the fastest-time record holder in all three races.

Ron Turcotte aboard Secretariat wins the Belmont Stakes.

Riva Ridge & EDDIE SWEAT & Secretariat

Eddie Sweat is **Riva Ridge**'s and **Secretariat**'s favorite guy. Often seen in his plaid or striped pants, Eddie is a groom for the two famous horses. Riva Ridge, the wire-to-wire winner of the 1972 Kentucky Derby and Belmont Stakes is known mostly because he is the stable mate of the great Secretariat. According to the horses' favorite jockey, **Ron Turcotte**, Eddie talks to the horses, forming a very special bond.

Eddie Sweat with Secretariat and Riva Ridge

Ron Turcotte on Riva Ridge with Eddie in striped pants.

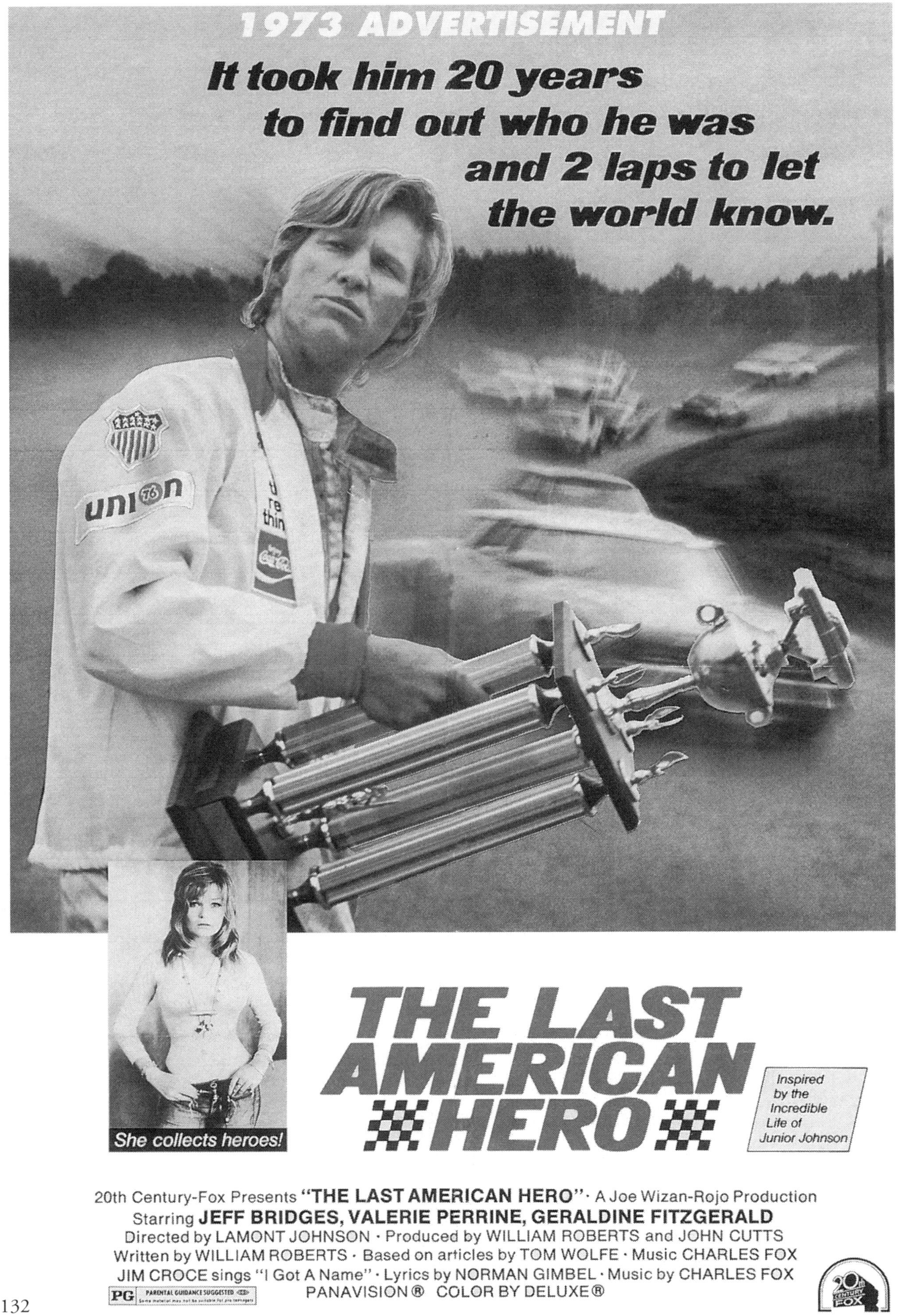

1973 ADVERTISEMENT

It took him 20 years to find out who he was and 2 laps to let the world know.

She collects heroes!

THE LAST AMERICAN HERO

Inspired by the Incredible Life of Junior Johnson

20th Century-Fox Presents **"THE LAST AMERICAN HERO"** · A Joe Wizan-Rojo Production
Starring **JEFF BRIDGES, VALERIE PERRINE, GERALDINE FITZGERALD**
Directed by LAMONT JOHNSON · Produced by WILLIAM ROBERTS and JOHN CUTTS
Written by WILLIAM ROBERTS · Based on articles by TOM WOLFE · Music CHARLES FOX
JIM CROCE sings "I Got A Name" · Lyrics by NORMAN GIMBEL · Music by CHARLES FOX
PANAVISION® COLOR BY DELUXE®

PG PARENTAL GUIDANCE SUGGESTED

horse racing

KENTUCKY DERBY • May 5

Secretariat, ridden by Ron Turcotte

PREAKNESS STAKES • May 19

Secretariat, ridden by Ron Turcotte

BELMONT STAKES • June 9

Secretariat, ridden by Ron Turcotte

HORSE OF THE YEAR

Secretariat

MONEY LEADER

JOCKEY

Laffit Pincay, Jr., 350 wins, 1444 mounts $4,093,492

Harness Horse of the Year

SIR DALRAE

Driver Ron Feagan

HOCKEY

art ross trophy

(LEADING SCORER)

Phil Esposito, Boston Bruins

calder memorial trophy

(ROOKIE OF THE YEAR)

Steve Vickers, New York Rangers

stanley cup champions

Montreal Canadiens over **Chicago Black Hawks** **4** games to **2**

hart memorial trophy

(MVP)

Bobby Clarke
Philadelphia Flyers

vezina trophy

(OUTSTANDING GOALIE)

Ken Dryden
Montreal Canadiens

lady byng memorial trophy

(MOST GENTLEMANLY PLAYER)

Gilbert Perreault
Buffalo Sabres

Montreal Canadiens

FOOT

SUPER BOWL VII

Dolphins fullback **Larry Csonka** evades Redskins Linebacker **Chris Hanburger** in Super Bowl VII.

1973 SUPER BOWL VII

MIAMI DOLPHINS
over
WASHINGTON REDSKINS
14-7

Super Bowl VII takes place on January 14, 1973, at Los Angeles Memorial Coliseum in Los Angeles to decide the National Football League (NFL) champions for the 1972 season. The American Football Conference (AFC) champion Miami Dolphins face the National Football Conference (NFC) champion Washington Redskins.

Boasting an undefeated 14-0 regular season and despite being shut out in the second half of a low-scoring game, the Dolphins stave off the Redskins for victory in their second Super Bowl appearance.

Super Bowl VII MVP: **Jake Scott**, Safety, Miami

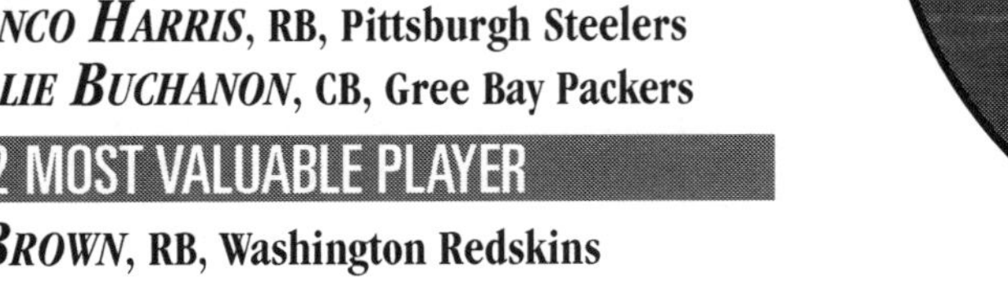

1972 NFL ROOKIE OF THE YEAR

Offense - *FRANCO HARRIS*, RB, Pittsburgh Steelers
Defense - *WILLIE BUCHANON*, CB, Gree Bay Packers

1972 MOST VALUABLE PLAYER

***LARRY BROWN*, RB, Washington Redskins**

BALL

Dolphins fullback **Larry Csonka** evades Minnesota Linebackers in Super Bowl VIII.

SUPER BOWL VIII

1974 SUPER BOWL VIII

MIAMI DOLPHINS over **MINNESOTA VIKINGS** 24-7

Super Bowl VIII takes place on January 13, 1974, at Rice Stadium in Houston, Texas to decide the National Football League (NFL) champions for the 1973 season. The American Football Conference (AFC) champion Miami Dolphins face the National Football Conference (NFC) champion Minnesota Vikings.

In their third consecutive Super Bowl appearance, the Dolphins dominate the Vikings, scoring 24 unanswered points in the first three quarters and relying primarily on their running game.

Super Bowl VIII MVP: **Larry Csonka**, Fullback, Miami

1973 NFL ROOKIE OF THE YEAR

Offense - *Chuck Foreman*, RB, Minnesota Vikings
Defense - *Wally Chambers*, DT, Chicago Bears

1973 MOST VALUABLE PLAYER

***O.J. Simpson*, RB, Buffalo Bills**

1973 ADVERTISEMENT

Schwinn . . . for the young in heart

Illustrated: The Schwinn 10-speed Varsity® Sport with fenders . . . $109.95, suggested price, slightly higher in some areas, subject to change without notice.

ONCE IN A LIFETIME THRILL

There's a once-in-a-lifetime thrill in store for you this Christmas morning when Santa drops off a new 10-speed Schwinn lightweight — it's a gift that keeps its Christmas spirit all year long . . . as you join the nearly 100 million cyclists who are re-discovering the carefree way of life. And with a genuine Schwinn bicycle you can be confident you're riding *the* quality bike with the quality name. Schwinn Dealers across the land are ready to serve you . . . and for safety's sake every Schwinn bike is assembled, adjusted and ready-to-ride at no extra cost. Schwinn bikes with gears . . . selections for the whole family, at your Schwinn Dealer now.

Send 25c for complete illustrated catalog

BICYCLE COMPANY

1860 NORTH KOSTNER AVENUE, CHICAGO, ILLINOIS 60639

Lightweights

Sting-Rays®

Exercisers

Unicycles

Tri-wheelers

Tandems

Racers

BASKETBALL

NBA Finals 1973

New York Knicks over Los Angeles Lakers

4 games to 1

FINALS **MVP**

Willis Reed Jr.
New York Knicks

In a rematch and exact reversal of the 1972 NBA Finals which saw the Lakers win in five games, 4-1, the Knicks turn the tables to earn their second NBA championship, 4-1 over the Lakers. The game is notable as the final game for storied Laker center **Wilt Chamberlain**, who scores the last points of the final game with one second remaining.

The Knicks

Heisman Trophy

HEISMAN TROPHY

John Cappelletti,
Penn State, Running Back

NATIONAL COLLEGE FOOTBALL CHAMPION

Alabama Crimson Tide

ROSE BOWL

USC Trojans over
Ohio State Buckeyes
42 - 17
MVP ***Sean Cunningham***,
USC, Running Back

NBA SCORING LEADER (Season)

Nate "Tiny" Archibald,
Kansas City/Omaha Kings 2,719

Nate Archibald

UCLA over Memphis State 87–66

• Most Outstanding Player •
Bill Walton,
UCLA

NBA FIELD GOAL PERCENTAGE (season)

Wilt Chamberlain,
Los Angeles Lakers, .727

NBA FIELD GOALS (points per game avg.)

Nate "Tiny" Archibald,
KC/Omaha Kings, 34.0

UCLA head coach **John Wooden** *— nicknamed the "Wizard of Westwood" — wins ten NCAA national championships in a 12-year period, including a record seven in a row and 5 in the '70s.*

NBA REBOUNDS (Season)

WILT CHAMBERLAIN
LA Lakers,
1526 (18.6 avg.)

ROOKIE OF THE YEAR

Bob McAdoo
Buffalo Braves

COACH OF THE YEAR

Tom Heinsohn
Boston Celtics

The **23rd NBA All-Star Game** is played at Chicago Stadium, with the **East beating the West 104-84. Dave Cowens** of the Boston Celtics is the MVP.

The **Cincinnati Royals** relocate and become the **Kansas City-Omaha Kings**, splitting home games between Kansas City, MO and Omaha, NE. And the **Baltimore Bullets** play their final season in Baltimore before moving to the Washington, D.C. suburb of Landover, MD, and becoming the **Capital Bullets**.

George Foreman defeats **Joe Frazier** in two rounds by a TKO to claim the World Heavyweight title. Although Foreman is undefeated, he is still a 3:1 underdog entering the fight. Frazier is undefeated as well. Broadcaster Howard Cosell memorably makes the pronouncement — "Down goes Frazier! Down goes Frazier!"

THE SUNSHINE SHOWDOWN

15 ROUNDS
WORLD HEAVYWEIGHT CHAMPIONSHIP
JOE FRAZIER
UNDEFEATED CHAMPION
VS
GEORGE FOREMAN
UNDEFEATED NO.1 CHALLENGER

A PROMOTION OF NATIONAL SPORTS LIMITED KINGSTON JAMAICA W.I.

JAMAICA

NATIONAL STADIUM KINGSTON JAMAICA • NO HOME TV

airJamaica official carriers

BOXING

HEAVYWEIGHT
George Foreman

MIDDLEWEIGHT
Carlos Monzon

WELTERWEIGHT
Antonio Cervantes

BANTAMWEIGHT
Arnold Taylor

January's Foreman-Frazier bout is the first telecast of HBO Boxing.

On March 31st, **Ken Norton** faces **Muhammad Ali** in a match for the NABF heavyweight title. Foreman wins the match, breaking Ali's jaw in the process. Ali has his revenge six months later, winning a split decision in a rematch at L.A.'s Forum.

tennis

U.S. OPEN

JOHN NEWCOMBE over **Jan Kodes**

MARGARET COURT over **Evonne Goolagong**

WIMBLEDON

JAN KODES over **Alex Metrevelli**

BILLIE JEAN KING over **Chris Evert**

FRENCH OPEN

ANDRÉS GIMENO over **Patrick Proisy**

BILLIE JEAN KING over **Evonne Goolagong**

AUSTRALIAN OPEN

ILLIE NASTASE over **Nikola Pilic**

MARGARET COURT over **Chris Evert**

DAVIS CUP

Australia over **USA, 5-0**

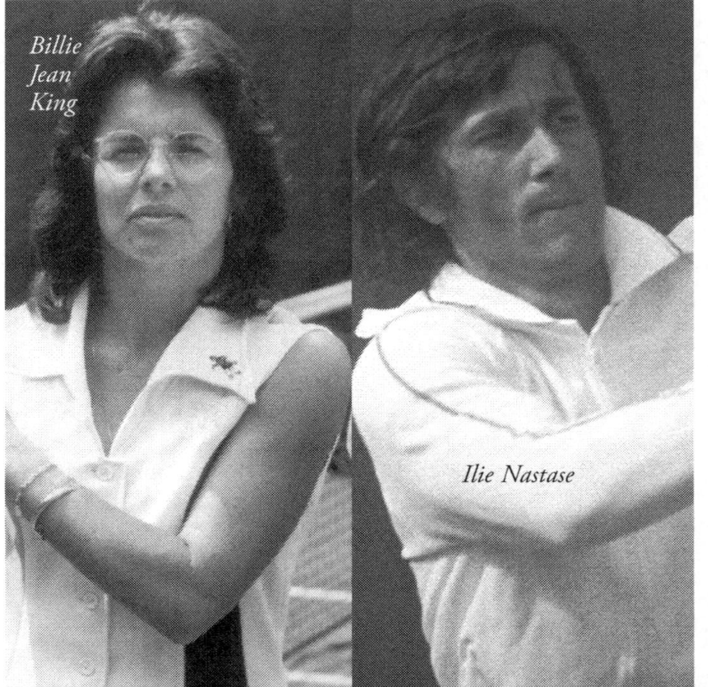

Billie Jean King

Ilie Nastase

golf

U.S. OPEN

Male .... JOHNNY MILLER
Female .... SUSIE BERNING

PGA / LPGA

Male .... JACK NICKLAUS
Female ...... MARY MILLS

PGA / LPGA LEADING MONEY WINNER

JACK NICKLAUS **$308,362**

KATHY WHITWORTH **$82,864**

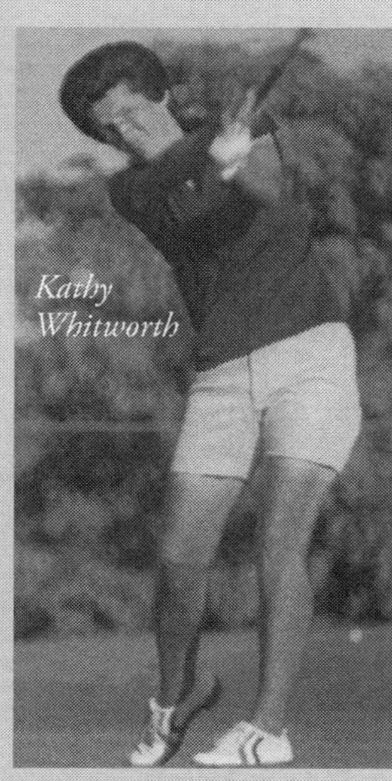

Kathy Whitworth

BRITISH OPEN

TOM WEISKOPF

MASTERS

TOMMY AARON

AMATEUR

U.S. .... CRAIG STADLER
British ..... DICK SIDEROWF

Johnny Miller

Tommy Aaron

Susie Berning

Jack Nicklaus

Cycling

TOUR de FRANCE

LUIS OCAÑA, Spain

Ocaña wins 6 cycling tournaments in 1973.

Boston Marathon

Winner

John Anderson
USA 2:16:03

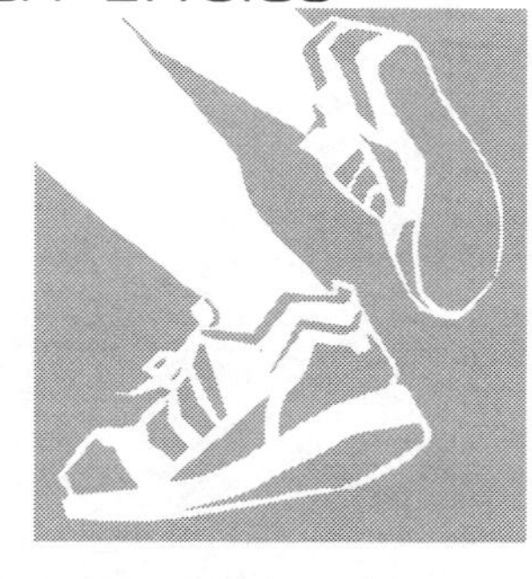

New York City Marathon Winners

Tom Fleming USA
2:21:54 (Course Record)

Nina Kuscsik USA
2:57:07 (Repeat Winner)

BOWLING

BPAA U.S. Open
Mike McGrath

PBA National Championship
Don McCune

In a year dubbed the "Year of the Soaker," McCune came to be known for chemically softening his bowling balls — a legal practice at the time.

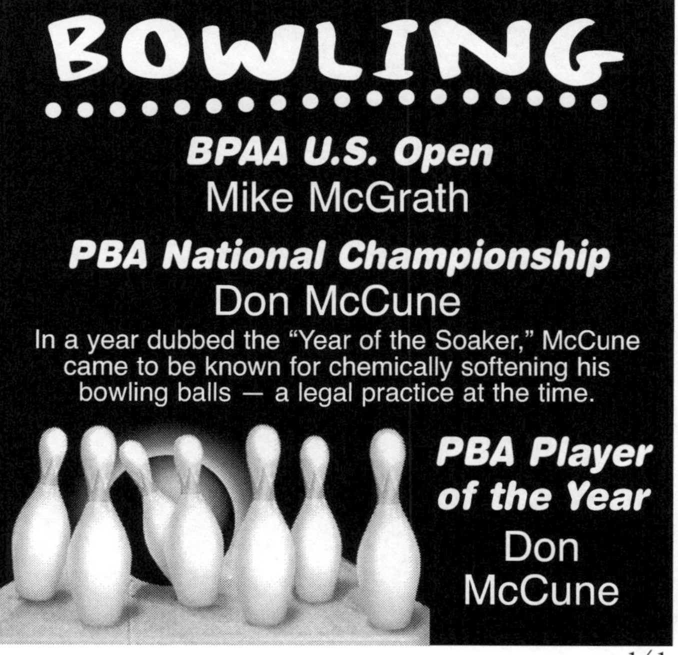

PBA Player of the Year
Don McCune

BORN in 1973

JASON ACUÑA ★ JUWAN HOWARD ★ OSCAR DE LA HOYA ★ MATT HUGHES ★ JASON KIDD ★ TERRELL OWENS ★ JALEN ROSE ★ JASON SCHMIDT ★ MONICA SELES ★ AMY VAN DYKEN ★ CHRIS WEBBER

Monica Seles

Terrell Owens

DIED in 1973

FRANÇOIS CEVERT, 29 RACE CAR DRIVER ★ RALPH EARNHARDT, 45 RACE CAR DRIVER ★ FRANKIE FRISCH, 74 BASEBALL PLAYER ★ GEORGE SISLER, 80 BASEBALL PLAYER ★ ROGER WILLIAMSON, 25 RACE CAR DRIVER

Frankie Frisch

French driver FRANÇOIS CEVERT dies in a crash during qualifying at Watkins Glen and British driver ROGER WILLIAMSON perishes in a fiery crash at the Dutch Grand Prix.

ASSORTED AWARDS

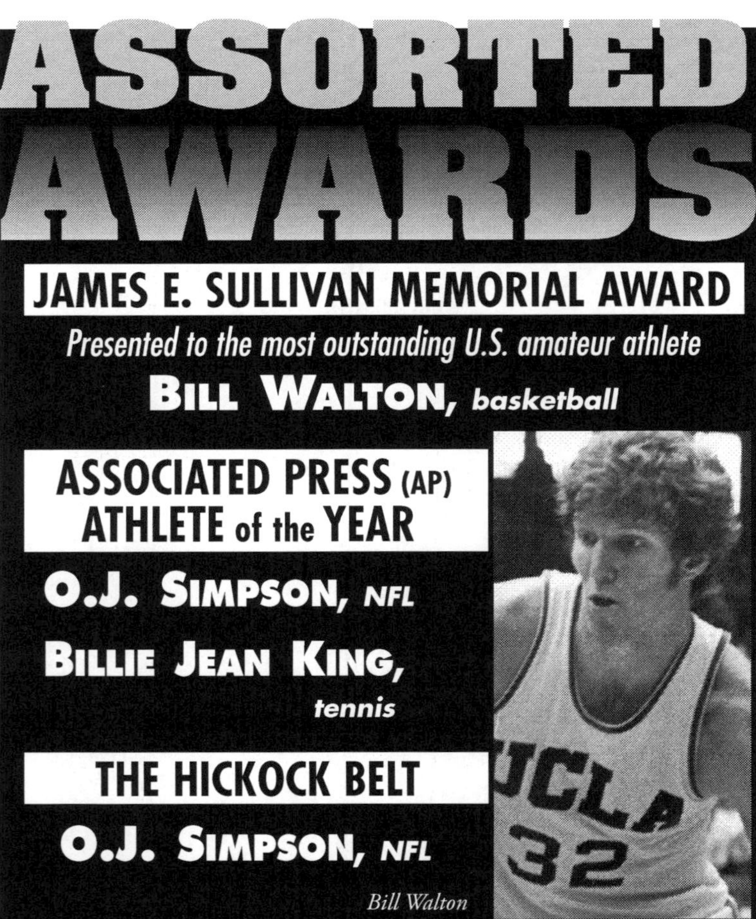

JAMES E. SULLIVAN MEMORIAL AWARD

Presented to the most outstanding U.S. amateur athlete

BILL WALTON, ***basketball***

ASSOCIATED PRESS (AP) ATHLETE of the YEAR

O.J. SIMPSON, ***NFL***

BILLIE JEAN KING, ***tennis***

THE HICKOCK BELT

O.J. SIMPSON, ***NFL***

Bill Walton

CHESS

REIGNING WORLD CHESS CHAMPION

BOBBY FISCHER, USA

In 1970 and 1971, FISCHER dominated chess to an extent never seen before, leading to his defeat of Boris Spassky to take the 1972 World Chess Championship title. The International Chess Federation rates him as the top player of 1973.

DOG SHOW

WESTMINSTER KENNEL CLUB Best in Show

Acadia Command Performance

Poodle - E. Jenner, J. Sering, *owners*

CAR RACING

INDIANAPOLIS 500

Winner
GORDON JOHNCOCK
159.036 mph avg. powered by an Offenhauser racing engine

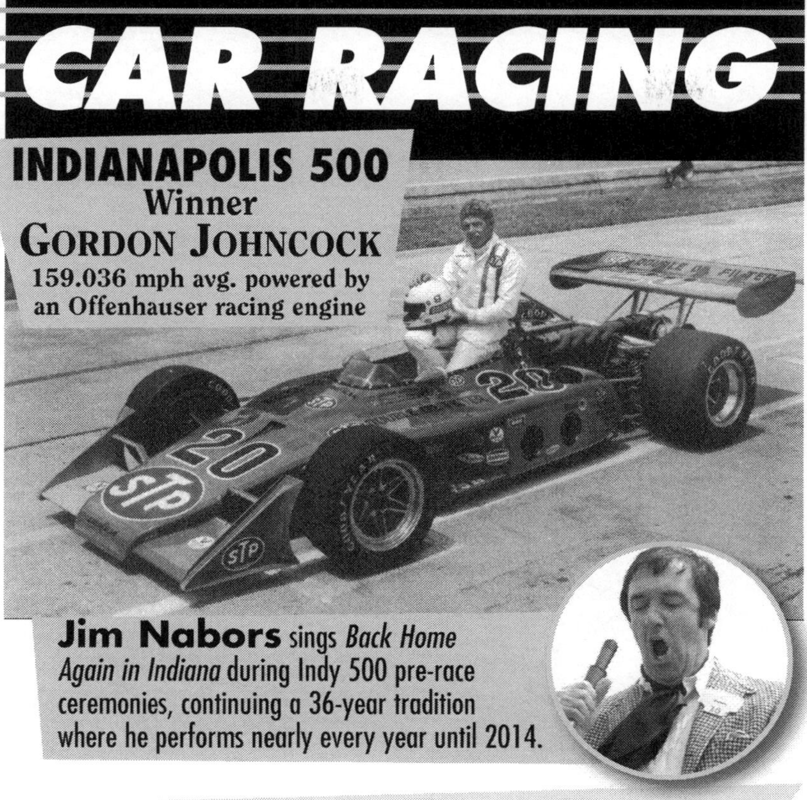

Jim Nabors sings *Back Home Again in Indiana* during Indy 500 pre-race ceremonies, continuing a 36-year tradition where he performs nearly every year until 2014.

24 Hours of LE MANS

HENRI PESCAROLO & HENRI PESCAROLO
Equipe Matra MS670B

MONACO GRAND PRIX

JACKIE STEWART

ITALIAN GRAND PRIX

RONNIE PETERSON

NASCAR WINSTON CUP CHAMPION

BENNY PARSONS

Figure Skating

WORLD CHAMPIONSHIPS

Men - **Ondrej Nepela** Czechoslovakia

Women - **Karen Magnussen** Austria

Pairs - **Irina Rodnina & Alexei Ulyanov** USSR

SKIING

ALPINE SKIING WORLD CUP

MEN'S OVERALL SEASON CHAMPION:
Gustav Thöni, Italy

WOMEN'S OVERALL SEASON CHAMPION:
Annemarie Pröll, Austria

Gustav Thöni

DISC SPORTS

Organized disc sports, in the 1970s, come into their own, beginning with promotional efforts from Wham-O. New tournaments include the Canadian Open Frisbee Championships (1972), Vancouver Open Frisbee Championships (1974), the Octad in New Jersey (1974), the American Flying Disc Open in Rochester, NY (1974), and the World Frisbee Championships in Pasadena, CA (1974).